T0330284

Understanding Muslim Philanthropy

Authors' Dedication Page

My mentors—Dwight Burlingame, Amir Pasic, Laurie Paarlberg, David Craig, Edward Curtis, Abdulkader Sinno, Mark Sidel, Angela Eikenberry, Alan Abramson, and so many more amazing colleagues from the Lilly Family School of Philanthropy, ARNOVA and ISTR communities.
My parents—Nasim and Sumera. For showing me the world and teaching me how to love its diversity. For collaborating to make the world a better place.
My siblings—Saima, Asher, Jawaad, Arshia, Maha, and Samee—for putting up with attempts to collaborate.
My children—Usama, Fatima, Amal, Safaa, and Zaki. For helping me recognize the beauty of how different people can collaborate to make the world better.
To my granddaughter—Raya Hanif. The world stops when you snuggle in my arms.
My wife—Sobia—my rock, my harbor, my day and night, my east and west, and my love.

– Shariq A. Siddiqui

Dad—who passed away too early but gave me everything and invested everything he had in my life so I could succeed. You are and will always be my Superman. I dedicate this book and all my life achievements to you.
Mom—for sacrificing everything, teaching me all I know, and always being my bedrock.
My siblings – Faraz, Sehrish, and Hareem—thank you for everything you have done for me.
My nephews and nieces—for all the joy you bring into my life every day.
My forever PhD Chair Aseem Prakash—thank you for believing in me when I did not even believe in myself, investing in me all your time, patience, and effort, and teaching me how to do high-quality research.
All the special people in my life—Hammad, Kate, Suma, Yusri, Omid, Wasil, Pam, Faisal, Siddharth, Yusri, Taylor, Megan, Tariq, Ali, Mirza, Riddhi, Rijul, Frankline—I owe this to you more than anyone else—thank you for bringing so much joy and happiness to my life.
To all the paramedics and unknown heroes who saved me after my drowning incident in 2018—more than anything, I owe you for this gift of life.

– Rafeel Wasif

To my parents, Stephen and Rosemary, for their unconditional love and support.
To my sister, Ellie Proudler, my brother-in-law, Jason, and my nephews, Elias and Ezra, who always remind me of the joys of family.
To the expansive Muslim Philanthropy Initiative team, for teaching me to think critically about philanthropy and to take seriously its role. Thank you for putting up with my incessant questions.
To my friends and mentors, I owe you a lifetime of thanks.
To those fighting for justice in a world of injustice, and for those in solidarity with struggles not their own, may we find hope together in the belief that another world is possible.

– Micah A. Hughes

Understanding Muslim Philanthropy

Shariq A. Siddiqui

Assistant Professor of Philanthropic Studies and Director of the Muslim Philanthropy Initiative, Lilly Family School of Philanthropy, Indiana University, USA

Rafeel Wasif

Assistant Professor in Public Administration and Nonprofit Management, Portland State University, USA

Micah A. Hughes

Associate Director, Center for Middle East and Islamic Studies, University of North Carolina at Chapel Hill, USA

Edward Elgar
PUBLISHING

Cheltenham, UK • Northampton, MA, USA

Published by
Edward Elgar Publishing Limited
The Lypiatts
15 Lansdown Road
Cheltenham
Glos GL50 2JA
UK

Edward Elgar Publishing, Inc.
William Pratt House
9 Dewey Court
Northampton
Massachusetts 01060
USA

A catalogue record for this book
is available from the British Library

Library of Congress Control Number: 2024939192

This book is available electronically in the **Elgar**online
Political Science and Public Policy subject collection
http://dx.doi.org/10.4337/9781035337293

ISBN 978 1 0353 3728 6 (cased)
ISBN 978 1 0353 3729 3 (eBook)

Printed and bound by CPI Group (UK) Ltd, Croydon, CR0 4YY

This book is dedicated to the John Templeton Foundation, whose generous grant, "A Muslim Philanthropy Network Engaging Faith, Religious Values and Spirituality for Social Good," has been instrumental in bringing this project to fruition. With profound gratitude, we acknowledge the Foundation's unwavering commitment to fostering dialogue, understanding, and action at the intersection of faith, philanthropy, and social impact. Your visionary support has empowered us to explore, articulate, and amplify the transformative potential of Muslim philanthropy in advancing positive change within our communities and beyond. May this dedication stand as a testament to our shared dedication to building a more compassionate, equitable, and interconnected world.

Contents

Introduction to *Understanding Muslim Philanthropy*

Indeed, Allah rewards the charitable.
Qur'an 12:88

This book started with early writings by Shariq Siddiqui during his graduate work at Indiana University Lilly Family School of Philanthropy and an article he published, "Muslim Philanthropy: Living Beyond a Western Definition," in the *Voluntary Sector Review*. These early writings led to a series of conversations with Rashid Dar at the John Templeton Foundation. These conversations ultimately led to a generous grant from the John Templeton Foundation to fund a research project called "A Muslim Philanthropy Network Engaging Faith, Religious Values and Spirituality for Social Good." This research project allowed a series of conversations and focus groups with Muslim philanthropists in the United States, Saudi Arabia, Qatar, United Arab Emirates, Malaysia, Indonesia, Pakistan, Ethiopia, Kenya, Jordan, South Africa, and Turkey, amongst other countries. An important meeting during this journey was at the "Faith and Philanthropy Summit" at the Vatican in collaboration with the Galileo Foundation and the World Congress of Muslim Philanthropists.

It was clear from these discussions that Muslim philanthropy was faced with a number of challenges. First, there was a rich history of charity, philanthropy, and social good within Islam and Muslim culture. This history and tradition had to engage with modern, largely Western ideas of philanthropy to seem "professional." In addition, Muslim philanthropy was being scrutinized due to the securitization of philanthropy as part of the Global War on Terror. However, it was also increasingly being seen as an opportunity to assist the state in fulfilling its social good obligations. Furthermore, Muslim philanthropy was being studied either as something within the prism of Islamophobia and the Global War on Terror or through a scientific philanthropy lens.

INTRODUCTION

This book seeks to locate and define contemporary Muslim philanthropy within the context of the rich and diverse history of Islamic practice and religious discourse on philanthropy. In doing so, this work not only interprets

Muslim philanthropy within the Islamic tradition, it also questions the universality of current definitions of philanthropy. Muslims represent nearly 1.6 billion of the global population. Their daily lives include charity, acts of kindness, good works, civic activities, and other acts that can be commonly understood as philanthropy. Why do Muslims carry out these activities—for the public good, for personal gain, for a just society, or for the love of God? What do these actions—or inactions—tell us about Muslims' understanding of their relationship to God and their fellow human beings? This book examines these questions in order to encourage readers to think more carefully and critically about the relationship between religion and philanthropy by making explicit the ways in which Muslim scholars, traditions, the general population, and practitioners have talked about and practiced charity. We focus specifically on how that history bears on Muslim philanthropy in the United States today.

Since September 11, 2001, the discourse about Islam in America has been steeped in debates and framed by issues of national security, terrorism, and the alleged incompatibility between Islam and democracy. The scrutiny of Muslim philanthropy has focused mainly on attacking or defending its role in national security, terrorism, and democracy. Academics who study Muslim philanthropy have sought to fit Islamic charitable practices within what is considered a "modern" definition of philanthropy. However, one popular and powerful contemporary definition—*voluntary action for the public good*—emerged in the context of Euro-American experiences largely framed in a secularized Christian discourse of poverty, charity, welfare, and volunteerism. This Euro-American definition precludes a more nuanced examination of Muslim philanthropy as a dynamic practice, ignoring the variety of social acts that constitute sadaqa, or Muslim charity. As this book will argue, a more expansive understanding of Muslim philanthropy is needed at the intersection of the study of religion and philanthropy in order to avoid misleading and limited analysis.

A Brief Overview of a Modern Definition

The *field* of philanthropic studies is an interdisciplinary field that initially grew out of the humanities and liberal arts. However, the *search for a definition* of philanthropy is much older. It frequently begins etymologically, starting in the fifth century BCE with the play *Prometheus Bound* in which Prometheus's character is described as "humanity loving." In this myth, Prometheus gives fire to the earliest proto-humans who had no means to develop culture. Fire symbolized technological advancement and civilization, a kind of "blind hope" or optimism for the future (Sulek 2010a). This connection to the ancient Greek play has been transformed through a mostly Western narrative as a central origin story of philanthropy, a story continually propagated via the scientific philanthropy movement, which has come to dominate the academic study of philanthropy's history. While Muslims also inherited and preserved ancient Greek traditions and developed, constructed, and spread novel charitable institutions such as endowments (Adam 2020; Makdisi 1981), the modern conception of philanthropy based in institutionalized (often secular) solutions to "causes" of human suffering (e.g., poverty) rather than the amelioration of "symptoms" (e.g., the suffering of the poor) have resulted in a narrow understanding of philanthropic traditions that do not fall neatly into these categories. One unfortunate result has been the displacement of certain alternative conceptualizations of charitable action and the social norms which undergird them.

With the embrace of Greek and Roman tradition, philanthropy became part of "civil religion" discourse. Historian Paul Veyne described the practice of *euergetism*, a Greek term used to refer to the expectation that the rich contribute from their wealth to help their community for the sake of prestige and honor (Veyne 1990). Similarly to the religious practices of tithing, euergetism was an established practice until it was replaced by more formal taxation (Isin and Lefebvre 2005; Nicholls 2020).

The historical narrative of philanthropy then moves to the late Middle Ages, the economic transformation of Europe, and the rise of cities as centers of communal life. Passage of the Charitable Uses Act of 1601 (the so-called Poor Laws) is considered a watershed moment in the legislation of philanthropy. It is considered as the first time "poverty was addressed in an organized and official way" (Payton and Moody 2008).

If we transition to early America, we see that the American colonies relied on the English model of governance and organization (Phillips and Jung 2016), which also affected the organization of charity. An analysis of the religiously grounded concern for the community in John Winthrop's sermon "A Model of Christian Charity" written in 1630, of Benjamin Franklin's support of community institutions through philanthropic contributions, and of the famous description of voluntary associations as a fixture of American civic life by Tocqueville, helped to further frame the uniquely American discourse of philanthropy (Hall 2006). These developments transitioned into the modern era through the scientific philanthropy movement that was promoted by people such as Andrew Carnegie and John D. Rockefeller (Bremner 1988). Missing from this historical exploration and development are other religious and cultural traditions, such as Islam.

Charity versus Philanthropy

There has long been a debate about the difference between philanthropy and charity. Philanthropy scholars have sought to define philanthropy as the preferred or higher form of social good. This distinction is best illustrated by the common refrain—charity is alleviating hunger by feeding someone a fish, while philanthropy is teaching someone how to fish. As Payton and Moody suggest:

> The common usage of charity versus philanthropy can be confusing … [P]hilanthropy is used primarily as an umbrella term for the entire spectrum of voluntary actions for the public good, while charity—which was at one time the umbrella term for the field—is used more narrowly. [T]he two terms are differentiated according to the two broad objectives of voluntary action mentioned earlier: philanthropy for acts to improve the quality of life versus charity for acts to relieve suffering … [I]f charity is a matter of bringing blankets and medicine and food to refugees, philanthropy is a matter of getting the refugee back home and putting their society back on the road to social and economic recovery. (2008, 38)

This distinction between charity and philanthropy begins to break down when we consider the various visions of charity enshrined in some religious traditions, like Islam, which frequently emphasize spiritual reward for intentional action (or abstention from harmful action) rather than achieving efficient outcomes, which are thought to be in the hands of God. Take, for example, the prophetic narrative (hadith) in which a man comes seeking guidance from the Prophet Muhammad on how to earn a place in heaven. He gives charity to a thief, prostitute, and undeserving man unwittingly. The Prophet suggests that the man must have faith in God as to what the final result of these acts might be.

A Muslim conception of philanthropy suggests that one can give charity to obtain approval from God. An example of this is found in Qur'an 2:271, "If you disclose your charitable expenditures, they are good; but if you conceal them and give them to the poor, it is better for you, and He will remove from you some of your misdeeds [thereby]. And Allāh, of what you do, is [fully] aware." Muslim philanthropy amplifies the importance of a person's intent. If the motivation behind giving is glory or material gain, it defeats the spiritual purpose of the gift. Many Muslims speak in terms of charity as a way to love God by doing public good (Mittermaier 2019; 2021).

Here the question for scholars of Muslim philanthropy should not be whether religious philanthropy is effective vis-à-vis other forms of altruistic behavior, but whether philanthropic acts rooted in religious practices and traditions have the same aims and or goals. Do they seek the *eradication of poverty* or more modest *alleviation of suffering experienced by the poor*? Obviously religious traditions have marshaled movements on behalf of both, but when efficacy becomes the only measure, the alternative logic that has historically motivated religious philanthropy can get lost, discarded, or ignored.

An additional challenge is that sometimes the alleviation of suffering leads to indirect improvements. For instance, take the work of the Indianapolis-based nonprofit Global Interfaith Program. They sought to help orphans and vulnerable children (OVC) by feeding them lunch. They quickly discovered this act of alleviating suffering resulted in test scores increasing and overall academic success for these children. We seek to question the philanthropy/charity distinction and argue that it often excludes religious action and favors secular modes of addressing the causes of social ills regardless of one's intention. Intention (niyya) is central for an individual Muslim's action in worship and social interaction. Thus, for the purposes of this study, we use the words charity and philanthropy interchangeably.

Global Philanthropy Debates and Muslim Philanthropy

But what about traditions of philanthropy with different genealogies than the Euro-American tradition described briefly above, not to mention alternative charitable practices such as those of enslaved Africans, African Americans, and indigenous peoples in the Americas? The study of charitable giving in the field of philanthropic studies and nonprofit research has almost exclusively focused on formal giving by primarily defining "giving" as philanthropic donations by households or individuals to nonprofit organizations (Bekkers and Wiepking 2011a; Fateh Ahmad and Majid 2021a; Heist et al. 2021; Wiepking 2021). Yet we know that this privileges only one type of philanthropic behavior in industrialized nations with highly developed institutions of civil society and a formalized, regulated third sector. For example, in many communities and developing countries, informal giving and person-to-person direct donations of time, money, and other goods to individuals outside of the donor's household form the bulk of charitable giving (Everatt et al. 2005). As a result, research on philanthropy often neglects various types of prosocial behavior, such as giving information and volunteering, that may be more common among the poor (Butcher and Einolf 2018; Heist et al. 2021; Penner et al. 2005).

This overemphasis on practices of philanthropy in the Global North leaves important gaps in our knowledge of how charity is practiced globally. For instance, in 2017, 71 percent of the articles published in *Voluntas* and 84 percent of those published in *Nonprofit and Voluntary Sector Quarterly* (NVSQ) originated from authors located in either North America or Western Europe (Ma and Konrath 2018). Furthermore, the few studies that focused on giving among the poor in the South sampled mostly urban populations (Kassam 2016; Lewis 1997; Wilkinson-Maposa et al. 2005; Wasif and Prakash 2017), whereas the majority of populations in the Global South live in rural areas.

Broader understandings of philanthropy are not simply about filling gaps in academic discussions, but concern our ability to engage in meaningful comparison across traditions, practices, and geographies (Wiepking 2021; Herzog et al. 2020). Comparative studies allow us to better understand the relationship between different social systems that influence philanthropic behavior worldwide (Barman 2017). Fortunately, the studies described here show that this is changing.

To better understand philanthropy, we need a more inclusive discussion of how different nations, cultural traditions, and languages define philanthropy (Fowler and Mati 2019). Studying philanthropy among populations traditionally underrepresented in this field requires a broadened comprehension of the subject. Fowler and Mati's (2019) conceptualization of African "gifting" demonstrated that Western interpretations often obscure prosocial behaviors embedded in uniquely African historical contexts. Similarly, Wilkinson-Maposa et al. (2005) developed the concept of "horizontal philanthropy" and addressed the moral or cultural norms that make many prosocial behaviors more obligatory than voluntary. Fowler and Mati (2019) used qualitative methods to document formal and informal volunteering behavior in the slums of Korogocho, Kenya. They found that volunteer behaviors in slums related to survival were aimed at mitigating the ubiquitous threat of insecurity by building layers of social capital. Kassam (2016) interviewed the urban poor of India and found that philanthropy is a give-and-receive relationship. They highlighted the importance of assisting relatives, the role of self-help groups (SHGs) as more formal venues to give, the practice of providing food, and the role of religion. All three studies offer insights into prosocial behaviors in what Fowler and Mati called "complex adaptive systems" of philanthropy (2019, 726).

Bringing these alternative perceptions of philanthropy to the forefront is important, because if we focus only on formal philanthropy in the West, we will fail to acknowledge how charitable practices mediate social relations, social responsibilities, and civic participation conceived otherwise. In particular, it enables us to study how philanthropy is practiced not only by the rich and the middle class of the Global North, but also by the poor and those living in the Global South. Thus, our interest here is to explore what other modes and traditions, both formal and informal, get lost when formalized giving is the only measure of philanthropy. What would it mean to conceive of philanthropy otherwise (Tunç 2022)?

UNDERSTANDING MUSLIM PHILANTHROPY

In this book we focus on three major Muslim philanthropic traditions: the waqf (religious endowments), zakat (obligatory giving), and sadaqa (optional religious giving). However, we argue that Muslim philanthropy extends beyond a historical or theological examination of these practices to analyze the role of formal institutions (such as INGOs and NPOs) and informal practices of direct giving, remittances, as well practices that Muslims consider acts of sadaqa but fall below the radar of philanthropic studies' definitions of charity and public good. These actions include simple intersubjective acts like smiling and encouraging others to do good as well as abstaining from causing harm and speaking out against injustice. While normative definitions in the study of philanthropy might not consider these charitable acts, in the Islamic traditions we attend to in this book, we argue that these constitute significant modes of Muslim charitable behavior that must be considered in order to extend philanthropy's definitional scope beyond those modes of religious philanthropy based in a Euro-American, largely Protestant, genealogy of charity. Regardless of the scholarly debates over definition, for centuries Muslims have practiced charitable, humanitarian, and social acts that can be described as philanthropy. Muslims draw on the Qur'an (the holy book of Islam), sunna (traditions of the Prophet Muhammad), and local traditions to influence their religious practices. Thus, the study of Muslim philanthropy is further complicated by the fact that Islamic law permits Muslims to assimilate local practices into Islamic practices, allowing regional variations in Islamic philanthropy.

We argue that Islamic philanthropy needs to be defined on its own terms. The book provides a theoretical framing of how to understand and assess philanthropy within the Muslim cultural and religious context. To do so, the authors examine rich scriptural sources (Qur'an and hadith) while simultaneously analyzing the contemporary Muslim "lived" context. Ultimately, this book provides a deeper understanding of the dynamic between Muslim faith and philanthropy.

However, writing one book on Muslim philanthropy is challenging because of the incredible diversity within these faith communities. Although there are unifying features for how this group of people practice their faith, there are many differences, due to ethnic, national, racial, geographic, and theological differences that play out in different political, cultural, and economic situations. In a recent book, *Philanthropy in the Muslim World: Majority and Minority Muslim Communities*, editors Siddiqui and Campbell (2023) argue, "While there may not be a single definition on what to call giving behavior among Muslims, there is agreement as to what informs this action. The Islamic faith provides guidance and direction to why they promote social work or community service." The editors argue against the popular understanding of the "Muslim World" and, for the purpose of their book, "redefine this idea, arguing that the Muslim world exists in any geographical context where Muslims live and practice their faith ... [and] purposely selected both Muslim majority and minority countries in this volume."

This volume, which comprises Muslims' giving practices in 18 Muslim majority and minority countries, illustrates a major challenge of writing about Muslim philanthropy in a contemporary context—the lack of empirical data.

Therefore, for the purpose of this current book, we start by exploring the broader complexities of Muslim philanthropy. We then select the Muslim minority community in the United States to examine how these practices may play out within a specific community. We selected Muslims in the United States because of the available empirical data through the work of the authors of this book, our research expertise, and because Muslims in the United States are highly diverse. They include people from every part of the world. While they include Black, Arab, Asian, Persian, Hispanic, Native American, and White people, no one group is a majority. It is a community in which nearly half were born outside the United States. We do not argue that this small community of 3.45 million "represents" Muslims in general, but that examining their behaviors through empirical research helps to inform our broader understanding of how a religious community may practice within a specific geographic, political, economic, and cultural context.

This book is divided into six chapters. Chapter 1, "What is Muslim Philanthropy?", argues that acts of beneficence and charity appear to be universal but the social and historical forms charitable actions take as well as the way they are discussed are culturally specific. This chapter raises the question of definitions: What is philanthropy? Is it the same everywhere? We argue that commonly used definitions of philanthropy in the field of philanthropic and nonprofit studies fail to account for the unique practices of Muslim philanthropy, which break down the binaries of public/private and voluntary/ obligatory that are so central to the modern definition of philanthropy used in scholarship today.

Chapter 2, "Studying Muslim Philanthropy through Data," examines the current state of data on global Muslim giving by conducting a broad literature review on Muslim philanthropy in existing international surveys and a specific focus on the giving practices of respondents in Pakistan, Turkey, Egypt, and Indonesia. We find several similarities and differences across the Muslim world. The results show several differences in altruism and generosity across the globe, as countries lie differently on a continuum of benevolence. We also find that religiosity is one of the primary drivers of philanthropy across the Muslim world. Additionally, factors like gender and social norms, such as marital status, wealth, education, and age, affect the motivation to give and the amount of money given. We also find that Muslims generally prefer giving to informal causes and are often hesitant to give to formal organizations.

Chapters 3 and 4 both take up the question of zakat from two unique vantage points. Chapter 3, "Zakat in Modern America," discusses the history of zakat, legal debates about its practice, and the way US-based Muslims understand and debate the topic of zakat today. We pay special attention to Muslim debates about modern institutions that collect and distribute zakat such as domestic and international NGOs (Save the Children, UNHCR, etc.) to understand how zakat is practiced as well as disputed. Chapter 4, "Beyond Religious Texts: Discussion of Zakat on Social Media," goes beyond traditional discourse based in religious texts to better comprehend everyday Muslims' understanding of philanthropy by looking at discussions of zakat on Twitter. We collected 100,000 tweets from Twitter and used a structural topical model (STM), an unsupervised machine learning model, to study the main topics around which Twitter users discuss zakat. Overall, we found that discussions of zakat, like mainstream philanthropy, often focus on its potential in how zakat will benefit both the receiver and the giver as it helps improve both the religious and moral standing of the giver while also helping the receiver. However, despite its potential, some users worry about the misuse of zakat and its use in corruption as well as promoting certain extremist groups.

Chapter 5, "The Practice of Sadaqa in Muslim America," analyzes the practice of voluntary or extemporaneous charity, called sadaqa. Unlike zakat, sadaqa can be given to any cause and is not mandatory. For this reason, sadaqa can be considered a mode of informal religious philanthropy. In this chapter, we consider three forms of US-based sadaqa practice: the first form is the sadaqa of enslaved African Muslims brought to the Americas who continued to engage in charitable behavior; the second is the mosque as a site of civic behavior and giving; the third form of sadaqa is general Muslim American practices of giving and volunteering based on original survey data.

The final chapter, "The Waqf: Evolution of an Institution," analyzes the institution of the waqf, or Islamic endowment. It begins with a historical overview of the institution, its origins in Islamic history and practice, and traces some of its key transformations in the modern period. While the waqf has been a central institution for the private financing of public goods, the waqf has also been an instrument of support for the extended family unit. This dual private and public usage has led scholars to debate its philanthropic and charitable merit. We examine these debates with the hope of demonstrating how the waqf's historical evolution has affected modern attempts to develop the waqf as an instrument of social finance and welfare. We trace this evolution into the contemporary US and ask how US-based NGOs and NPOs have used the waqf as a model while distancing themselves from some of the legal and historical traditions of the past.

1.   What is Muslim philanthropy?[1]

> And among them are those who made a covenant with Allah, [saying], "If He should give us from His bounty, we will surely spend in charity, and we will surely be among the righteous."
>
> Qur'an 9:75

A SHORT HISTORY OF PHILANTHROPY

Philanthropy is ubiquitous, ranging, for example, from individual donors to family foundations, to endowments that support long-term giving programs for specific causes, to large nonprofit foundations that support other nonprofits through grants or other assets, and government and nongovernment grants that help sustain public programs. Thus, philanthropy can take many forms. Our contemporary understanding of the word has largely been defined by pointing to the world's wealthiest individuals, such as Bill Gates, George Soros, Warren Buffett, and MacKenzie Scott (Benthall 2017). In this understanding, philanthropy is what the über-rich do with their excess wealth. Moreover, this kind of philanthropy is institutional; wealthy businesspeople create institutions designed to provide financial resources to support various causes, as in the case of the Bill and Melinda Gates Foundation, whose stated goal is to combine private wealth with public service to provide solutions to global problems. Few look to ordinary individuals such as parents, community elders, or friends who are working to strengthen their communities by donating their time and money. Even fewer look to communities of color or marginalized groups for a deeper understanding or model of philanthropic practice (Freeman 2020; Johnson 2017; Pope and Flanigan 2013). Contemporary definitions of philanthropy and the field of philanthropic studies were developed primarily by building upon scholarship focused on the Global North, even as powerful organizations such as the Carnegie and Ford Foundations were expanding the hegemony of American philanthropy in Africa and elsewhere, leaving questions about diverse experiences of philanthropy and alternative practices unaddressed and their key concepts uninterrogated (E. H. Berman 1983; Fisher 1983; Karl and Katz 1987; Morey 2021; Mueller 2013).

By some accounts, the word philanthropy dates to the Greek myth of *Prometheus Bound* in the fifth century BCE. In this story, the gods are displeased with Prometheus for transgressing the will of Zeus by giving the privilege of fire to humankind out of kindness and concern for humanity, that is, due to his philanthropic character (*philanthrôpou trópou*). From this perspective, philanthropy is an act of rebellion out of "love of humanity." This is a common understanding of the term in which some inner motivation—love, pity, kindness, or ego—inspires someone to donate their time or money for the benefit of another. Yet the contemporary practice of philanthropy derives as much, if not more, from the legal, political, and economic transformations of the twentieth-century world as it does from ancient Athens. Despite its ancient Greek etymological origin, contemporary usage of the term has a modern pedigree that has both expanded and transformed philanthropy as an idea and a practice (Sulek 2010a; 2010b). Philanthropy's organizational and institutional structure often means that it is placed in opposition to the more informal and extemporaneous nature of charitable giving, which has been the predominate form of altruism for all but wealthy and powerful elites. The early twentieth century saw the rise of the "scientific philanthropy movement," partly as a critique of modern Christian charity (caritas) as ineffective at addressing root causes and partly as the creation of a new sector of bourgeois social activism made possible by heretofore unseen amounts of accumulated wealth, power, and prestige (Benthall 2017; Soskis 2014; Zunz 2014). Taken together, this narrative portrays a process in which philanthropy became centrally organized, professionalized, privatized, and secularized.

This story grows more complicated when we turn to religious philanthropy. The word philanthropy in the modern sense of individual or institutional voluntary action does not exist as such within foundational textual traditions of most religions. Jewish, Christian, Islamic, Sikh, and Hindu traditions include practices that may fit well within modern scholarly definitions of philanthropy (Eck 2013; Murphy 2004), yet the concepts and practices within each belong to very different discursive traditions and fields of practice (Asad 1986; Bourdieu 1991). Religious traditions like Islam and Sikhism have various charitable practices, such as sadaqa and seva, respectively, that one *could translate* into contemporary notions of charity or philanthropy, but also extend beyond the modern confines of those concepts to a larger terrain of practices and belong to what anthropologist Talal Asad, drawing from the philosopher of language, Ludwig Wittgenstein, has called different "conceptual grammars" (Asad 2003; Iqbal and Odabaei 2021; Moumtaz 2021).

However, this ancient idea of "love of humanity" was not an abstract or general love devoid of communal specificity or mythological context, especially for those living in antiquity; it was always contextualized and embedded in the narratives and social practices, or forms of life, of those communities engaged in philanthropy. Contemporary scholarly definitions of philanthropy narrate the origins of their field from this history but do so under completely different social, economic, and political conditions.

In the fields of philanthropic and nonprofit studies, leading scholars such as Salamon, Van Til, Payton, McCully, Billis, and others have laid the groundwork for defining modern philanthropy and philanthropic movements (Sulek 2010a). One popular definition is "voluntary action for the public good," which was coined by Robert Payton of the Indiana University Center on Philanthropy in an effort to promote the establishment of philanthropy as an academic discipline based on more than a century of historical and policy research on civil society and philanthropy in the United States (Hall 1999). Another popular academic definition developed by Salamon (1999) defines philanthropy as "the private giving of time or valuables (money, security, property) for public purposes" (10). Van Til (1990) defines philanthropy as "the voluntary giving and receiving of time and money aimed (however imperfectly) toward the needs of charity and the interests of all in a better quality of life" (34). All these definitions treat money, time, and wealth directed toward notions of public good as key components of philanthropy. McCully (2008; 2012) seeks to broaden this definition to include "private initiatives for the public good, focusing on quality of life" (13). However, his synthesis remains focused on formal organizations and voluntary action. These definitions tend to evoke the voluntary rather than the obligatory, the individual-institutional nexus of civil society over state actors and intervention. David Billis (2020) adds community and family to the mix in an attempt to rethink philanthropy beyond the civil society–state dichotomy. These framings of philanthropy, which narrate a story from Greco-Roman origins through medieval charity to the transformations of the scientific philanthropy movement at the beginning of the twentieth century, all tend to ignore the informal relational side and prioritize a social-scientific definition (Klopp 2015; McCully 2012). Modern philanthropy has narrowed its focus on specific practices (e.g., giving time and money) that cannot—and perhaps are not meant to—account for the rich expansive history of philanthropy, especially traditions that do not assume the charity versus philanthropy distinction.

These definitions need to be reframed and adapted in order for us to include forms of religious philanthropy that expand beyond congregational giving and address philanthropic-religious traditions beyond secularized, Western Christian practices. For the purpose of this chapter, we seek to broaden the understanding of philanthropy to account for philanthropic practices that sit uneasily within the current literature and scholarly foci. In the book, we argue that the broad field of Muslim philanthropy is precisely one charitable tradition that fits uneasily in these dominant definitions of philanthropy as well as under the generalized category of "religious giving" or "religious philanthropy."

ISLAM AND PHILANTHROPY

Because researchers exploring Muslim philanthropy in the past have tended to look for practices that fit within a Western-centric definition, they overemphasize donating money or time at the expense of other activities. Therefore, scholars of Islam and Muslim societies have focused their understanding of Muslim philanthropy mainly on the financial components of waqf (endowments), zakat (almsgiving), and sadaqa (charity). Here, the challenge is not whether there is a distinct "Western" or "Muslim" practice of philanthropy, but rather in privileging an idea of philanthropy that relies heavily or exclusively on definitions rooted in one particular historical and cultural experience at the expense of others, such as the charity–philanthropy distinction that emerged out of the modern "scientific philanthropy movement."

Searching for a Definition

There are a number of terms found in the Qur'an that are often understood to be examples of a more expansive notion of religious philanthropy. These include *zakat*, *sadaqa*, *birr* (righteousness), *amal al-salihat* (good deeds), *khayr* (goodness), and *ihsan* (virtue) (Fauzia 2013, 32). The precise legal and theological nature of these evolving concepts and practices challenge contemporary definitions of philanthropy that insist on the "voluntary" nature of modern charity, driven by an *individual* concern for common wellbeing or public good.

Zakat is perhaps the most paradigmatic example of Muslim charity. Jonathan Benthall (1999) has called zakat an act of "financial worship" bridging the category of financial welfare (such as aid to the poor) and ritual worship (Arabic: 'ibadat). For example, if an interested reader wanted to find information about how, when, and where one should give zakat, they would most likely consult a religious scholar in their community who has studied various jurisprudential texts (fiqh) and schools of thought (madhahib) in the Islamic tradition. Interestingly, the section on zakat rules would be found under the section on "worship" ('ibadat) rather than the section on "social transactions" (mu'amalat). This understanding of zakat as a ritual act as well as a welfare practice has led some scholars (Hanif 2022; Mattson 2010; Singer 2008) to insist that zakat has historically functioned more like a tax under Muslim polities, and yet, many contemporary Muslims speak about zakat as an act of religious philanthropy (Siddiqui et al. 2022).

While these categories are broad, Islamic jurisprudential scholarship has elaborated on the application of these categories throughout history and they remain a topic of considerable debate today (Abraham 2018; Kuran 2003;

Mahajneh, Greenspan, and Haj-Yahia 2021; Qaradawi 2020a; 2020b). Zakat can be used for the poor (al-fuqarā') and needy (al-masakīn), for employees of zakat administration (al-ʿamilīn), for evangelizing Islam (al-mūʾalafati qulūbu-hum), for freeing captives (al-riqāb), for freeing people in debt (al-ġarimīn), for the cause of God (fī sabīl Allah), and for helping travelers (ibn sabīl). In addition, the Qurʾan states that this is an obligation (al-farīḍa) given by God.

Zakat is often analogized to the Christian tithe, even though it remains distinct in its theological-legal formulation and social application. The Qurʾan defines zakat as an act of purification and growth (Singer 2008, 36). The first meaning suggests that by giving a fixed proportion of one's wealth, the remainder of that wealth is purified. Growth signifies God's promise to multiply the giver's generosity. Zakat, which is one of the five obligatory pillars of Muslim ritual belief and practice, is sometimes referred to as an "alms-tax." Some historians of Islam, such as Singer (2008; 2018) and Mattson (2010), argue that certain Muslim charitable acts are not philanthropy in the modern sense of the term, but rather religious obligations that have been historically more akin to a tax in which a Muslim polity collects zakat as a religious duty incumbent on all eligible Muslims, while non-Muslim subjects pay a separate tax in return for military exemption. For example, Ingrid Mattson (2010) argues that in the past the state collected and distributed these funds. Analogously, Robert Payton argues that since tithing in Christianity is obligatory, it does not fall within the voluntary nature of philanthropy. He similarly notes that, as one of the five pillars of Islam, zakat is not voluntary, and that Muslims are required to pay 2.5 percent of their surplus wealth and assets to specific causes.

The medieval Catholic Church and Catholic kingdoms viewed the tithe as a form of taxation collected by and given to the church to finance its operations and various campaigns (such as the Saladin Tithe during the Crusades) (Grzymała-Busse 2023, 90–98). In this case, the tithe was largely indistinguishable from state and feudal taxation and may have operated in a manner much closer to medieval Muslim policies around state zakat collection. Yet, for many American Protestant churches in the nineteenth century, a new language of an individual Christian tithe emerged, emphasizing giving directly to one's local congregation as an act of stewardship (King 2018). Protestant church leaders influenced by the scientific philanthropy movement adopted a new type of pastoral "professionalism" and thus modeled their tithe policies on business practices (King 2018). The new language around American tithing practices further differentiates the tithe from zakat which is not given to the mosque, even if the mosque serves as a site of collection and distribution.

Sadaqa is a general term for charitable and pious actions, and in the Qurʾan, the word is broadly used to encompasses all forms of giving, both obligatory, like zakat, as well as voluntary. Yet, it also has a distinct reference, which distinguishes it from zakat. In its more specific definition, sadaqa means informal, nonobligatory acts of charity that one is encouraged to do. The Hebrew term *sedaka* (or *tzedakah*) and the Arabic term sadaqa are cognates and both derive from the Semitic root /sdk/, meaning right, privilege, grant, or gift (Singer 2008, 5). Both in Arabic and Hebrew, the word has a strong connection to notions of justice. However, Muslims who fail to give sadaqa are not committing a sin, but they are promised great religious rewards if they engage in this voluntary practice. There are no limitations on sadaqa, and it is presumed that most non-zakat extemporaneous forms of charity by Muslims fall within this category, including both required and voluntary forms. It is under this expansive definition that even a smile can be an act of philanthropy.

The third institutionalized form of philanthropy is the waqf, or endowment. The waqf originated from a hadith when Umar ibn al-Khattab, the second Caliph who reigned from 634–44 CE, acquired a property and asked the Prophet whether he should donate it to charity (Sanjuán 2007, 58; J. N. D. Anderson 1951; Gil 1998). The Prophet replied, "Encumber the things itself and devote its fruits to pious purposes." Umar instructed that the property could not be sold, and its income was to be donated to specific charitable purposes. Thus, a waqf is a form of perpetual charity designed to give long after the initial donation takes place. Waqfs exemplify where Muslims transformed an existing local practice and institutionalized it in the practice of their faith (Cizakca 2000, 233).

The following hadith further illustrates how Muslim philanthropy goes beyond giving of time, treasure, or talent. The Prophet Muhammad reportedly stated, "Every Muslim has to give for charity." They asked, "O Prophet of Allah, how about one who has nothing to give?" He said, "He should work with his hands and benefit himself and also give in charity." They said: "If one cannot do even that?" He replied: "He should help one who is eager to have help." They said: And if he could not do that?" He answered: "Then he should do good action and abstain from evil, this is a charity for him" (Bukhari n.d.). Thus, all Muslims can participate in the benefits of philanthropy. Those who can afford to do so, can give of their wealth, those who have nothing and can give nothing can give charity by refraining from doing evil deeds. Thus, Muslim notions of philanthropy include voluntary *inaction* for the public good, as well. Modern Western definitions of philanthropy (such as those by Payton, Salaman, and Van Til) emphasize the giving of time and money. Muslim notions of philanthropy emphasize limiting or abstaining from harmful actions in addition to proactive benevolent actions. Philanthropy in Islam is not just about the benefits that society gets from charity but also about the development of a certain kind of human subject who has developed their capacities in line with the values and norms of the Islamic tradition. Central to this conception of the human subject is compassion and charity. Just as important as the giving is the effect that giving has on the donor. The acts seek to draw individuals closer to God through transformation of oneself by transforming those around them.

These scholarly debates seek either to define Islamic scripture or to capture Muslim practice over time. As discussed, scholars and practicing Muslims may disagree on how some of these religious requirements, such as zakat, are to be practiced. Muslims draw on stories from the life of the Prophet Muhammad and also scripture from the Qur'an and the sunna. Muslim philanthropic obligations and their corresponding effects are often discussed with reference to the here-and-now (alleviating the suffering of the poor) as well as the benefits that accrue in the hereafter.

While there is no single word that can easily translate philanthropy into the Arabic language sources of Islamic law and theology, scholars McChesney (1995) and Fauzia (2013) argue that, in the Qur'an, philanthropy is understood to mean Muslims' moral obligation to do good for God. As we have noted, the study of Muslim philanthropy is complicated by the many sects and their different schools of thought within Islamic law, permitting Muslims to assimilate local practices into their religious behaviors and allowing regional variations in Muslim philanthropy. For example, Diouf (1999; 2022) illustrates how enslaved African women baked rice cakes, or saraka (which comes from the Arabic sadaqa), as a form of charitable worship and to maintain their Muslim identity in spite of pressured conversion to Christianity and the inhumane conditions of slavery in the Americas. At a time when enslaved people were not allowed to practice their faith openly or in private, these women sought to interpret, transform, and implement a form of sadaqa. We argue, following Diouf, that this act should be seen as a unique Muslim-American expression of Muslim philanthropy.

More recently, Muslims have sought to develop their own framing of Islamic philanthropy that may not easily reconcile with scholarly definitions in the literature today. According to the recorded sayings and doings of the Prophet Muhammad (hadith), any act of goodness is considered sadaqa. Smiling, stopping oneself from saying or doing something that will cause harm, volunteering, donating to any charitable cause, or helping another person are all included as acts of charitable worship considered sadaqa.

For example, a recent study suggests that Muslim Americans' definitions of charity and philanthropy go beyond the giving of money and time to include actions found in the prophetic traditions (Siddiqui et al. 2022).

Islamic Jurisprudence and Muslim Diversity

Like many religious traditions, Muslims are geographically, culturally, linguistically, and theologically diverse. Muslims are an estimated 1.9 billion individuals, or nearly 25 percent of the world's population (Pew Research

Center 2011). And yet, Western media (via news, television, movies, etc.) often depict Islam as a unified, monolithic, and static tradition, and Muslims as univocal; the demographic and sociological reality is much more complicated. The Islamic tradition is defined as much by what Muslims agree on as by what they debate and contest. Importantly, the sociological fact of this diversity is acknowledged in the most central text of Islamic belief and practice, the Qur'an. In one often quoted verse, it states, "O mankind, indeed We have created you from male and female and made you peoples and tribes that you may know one another. Indeed, the most noble of you in the sight of Allāh is the most righteous of you. Indeed, Allāh is Knowing and Aware" (Qur'an 49:12). This acknowledgment of the diversity and differences of humanity is perhaps an initial reminder about the multiplicity of life ways through which people live and express their norms and commitments. While this Qur'anic verse suggests an acknowledgment that human beings share in a common humanity, they were not created as a monolithic group. One important consequence of this view is that difference is something to be understood, valued, and negotiated, rather than overcome, especially when it manifests in diverse expressions of religious experience, culture, and philanthropic acts that could fulfill one's religious obligations.

Furthermore, Muslims have clear theological diversity. Take, for example, two of the largest traditions of Islamic belief and practice—Sunni and Shiite. Each has multiple, competing schools of thought that pertain to theological beliefs as well as worship practices ('ibadat) and social transactions (mu'amalat). However, there are countless other groups of Muslim believers, including 'Ibadi, Ismaili, Moorish Science Temple, Nation of Islam, Ahmadiyya Movement in Islam to name only a few. Not every group is accepted or acknowledged by other Muslim groups. This diversity is heightened because even within these traditions, there are additional schools of theological argument and modes of practice. For example, Sunni Muslims, which are the largest tradition of Muslims, includes several schools of jurisprudence (fiqh), including Hanafi, Maliki, Shafi'i, and Hanbali—all of which are recognized as legitimate by the others despite their differences in legal rulings. This diversity is not unique to Sunni Muslim thought and practice but can be found across Islamic traditions broadly. For example, the second largest Muslim tradition, Shi'ism, similarly includes various schools of legal thought, with several groups that share historical narratives, but differ in organizational structure and contemporary practice. Therefore, no one book, scholar, or interpretive tradition can comprehensively illustrate the diverse religious practice of Muslims, which has deep implications for Muslim philanthropy.

A brief overview of Sunni Islamic legal theory

Historian of Sunni Islamic jurisprudence Wael Hallaq (1997) suggests that Islamic legal theory recognizes a variety of sources and methods through which Islamic normative judgments can be derived. It is important in this discussion of Islamic jurisprudence to understand why the Qur'an is not the only source of Islamic law, and as a result, cannot be the only source consulted when examining practices of Muslim philanthropy. Islamic scholars often make a distinction between Islamic jurisprudence (fiqh), which is the human discursive tradition of interpreting divine law, and the shari'a, which are those divine rulings commanded by God as well as a source of guidance for its followers. In short, Islamic jurisprudence is the interpretive act of identifying, categorizing, and applying the legal rulings made clear in the Qur'an and elaborated on in the sayings and actions (sunna) of the Prophet Muhammad.

Islamic jurisprudence was formalized into various schools over several centuries after the death of the Prophet Muhammad. Additionally, the Prophet Muhammad's actions and how his closest companions, the early community, and the succeeding two generations interpreted his actions (recorded in the hadith literature) also constitute a source of authoritative knowledge for Muslims. In fact, a study of the four major Sunni schools of jurisprudential thought shows how much of its development took place in the subsequent generations after the death of Prophet Muhammad (Zahrah 2001). Imam Malik ibn Anas of Medina (712–795), Abu Hanifa of Kufa (687–767), Muhammad ibn Idris as-Shafi'i of Mecca (767–820), and Ahmad ibn Hanbal of Baghdad (780–855) were the eponymous founders of the major schools of legal thought within Sunni Islam. The work of these four scholars and their students resulted in legal thought organized into schools over the succeeding centuries that the many Muslims identify with today (Bassiouni and Badr 2001, 142). Therefore, Sunni jurisprudence considers the period of the Prophet Muhammad's life, the lives of his followers, and the rule of the first four caliphs—or political successors Abu Bakr, Umar, Uthman, and Ali—as the period that shaped the formation of Islamic law.

Importantly, the major of schools of jurisprudence across various Muslim theological traditions developed elaborate interpretative practices and precedents to govern legal rulings. As schools of jurisprudence formed into distinct, independent bodies shape from the ninth to the thirteenth centuries CE, they also developed school-wide doctrines (juristic preferences and precedents) and began to rely on certain privileged legal texts and maxims which were used to communicate their positions on a range of topics as well as to train new generations of scholars. This complex development of Islamic law provided the flexibility Muslim populations needed to develop sets of rules on which they could rely, and which has increased religious diversity in Muslim communities globally.

For the Islamic legal scholar, the following four sources constitute an authoritative framework for deriving normative principles about how one should act and worship. For Sunni Muslims this meant relying on the theological authority of textual traditions as well as the use of rationality to develop logical deductions and methods. These included the Qur'an as the primary source of guidance and law, followed by the hadith, which are records of the sunna or the Prophet Muhammad's exemplary sayings, doings, and specific actions of which he approved or disapproved. The hadith compendiums were narrated via lines of transmission by the Prophet's companions (Hallaq 1997; 2005, 43–49; Nyazee 2000). The sunna derives its authority from the Qur'an itself (Bassiouni and Badr 2001, 150). The Qur'an constantly commands Muslims to obey not only God but also his last messenger, Muhammad. The sunna was not codified in written form during the Prophet Muhammad's life. However, in later years, many compilations were produced of which two are commonly considered to be the most authoritative by Sunni Muslims: Sahih Bukhari and Sahih Muslim. The sunna is secondary to the Qur'an and therefore may not contradict or change Qur'anic injunctions but may be used to illuminate any ambiguities found therein.

But what should Muslims do in cases where the Qur'an and the sunna do not address a particular issue or situation? In such cases, Islam provides additional sources that can be considered secondary sources of Islamic law. There are differing opinions regarding the exact number of secondary sources. However, for the sake of this discussion, for the purpose of comparison, and to gain a broader understanding of Islamic law, the list will be inclusive rather than exclusive.

• The first secondary source is ijmā', or consensus (Nyazee 2000; Hallaq 2005). This source comes directly from the Prophet Muhammad, who believed that his community would never agree in error. Ijma has been accepted by scholars as a component of Islamic law.
• The next secondary source is qiyas, or reasoning by analogy (Hallaq 1989, 287–8). This source requires jurists to investigate the specific reasoning behind certain rulings (ahkam) and to discover whether any analogies can be drawn for other cases. Qiyas requires a jurist to determine the rationale of an earlier decision and then use that rationale in the case at hand. Technically, qiyas is a form of logical syllogism requiring the derivation of a conclusion through the use of two known premises (Nyazee 2000; Hallaq 1990). An example of the use of qiyas occurred when scholars prohibited narcotics. They analogized that alcohol is prohibited because of its physically intoxicating qualities. Since narcotics are also intoxicating, they are also prohibited (Bassiouni and Badr 2001).

- Urf, or custom, is another source of Islamic law (Abu-Shamsieh 2020, 91–2). When a law, tradition, or custom exists within a community that is compatible with other sources of Islamic law, it is not rejected simply because it is derived from sources outside of the Qur'an and sunna. Customs exist to guide communities beyond what is expected of them in terms of Islamic legal norms and rulings.
- Maslaha, or the common good, is another significant tool in the practice of Islamic jurisprudence, especially in the modern period. Muslim jurists have identified five aims (maqasid) of Islamic law, namely, the securing of one's faith, life, intellect, progeny, and wealth. Scholar of Islamic Law, Felicitas Opwis, states that "the concept of maslaha can serve as a vehicle for legal change. It presents jurists with a framework to tackle the problem, inherent in a legal system that is based on a finite text, of bringing to bear the limited material foundation of the law (i.e., Qur'an and hadith) on everyday life in an ever-changing environment. It thus bestows legitimacy to new rulings and enables jurists to address situations that are not mentioned in the scriptural sources of the law" (Opwis 2005, 183).

Muslim Philanthropy: Tensions and Challenges

Muslim philanthropy has been shaped by the location and historical period in which it was practiced. For example, at the time of the Prophet Muhammad, all Muslims within the kingdom governed by him were required to pay zakat. However, waqfs were not administered by the state. During the time of Muslim rule in Spain, the waqf had become an important instrument of political legitimacy and power (Sanjuán 2007, 58). The waqfs, while endowed by private individuals, were administered by local judges (qadis). Despite this political gain, scholars have argued that the primary reason for these forms of religious endowments were personal salvation (Lev 2005, 1). While philanthropic foundations like the waqf were considered an important tool of state control, they were also vital for Muslim civil society. Because of this latter role, the British and French colonialists of Muslim lands treated this form of Muslim philanthropy with hostility (Çizakça 2000, 233).

Philanthropy has been equally important to men and women. However, philanthropy provided Muslim women with a rare vehicle to participate in public displays of power during the Ottoman period (Singer 2008, 127). For most of Muslim history, philanthropy has remained in the realm of private individuals. These acts can be seen through the waqfs that have been established across the world wherever Muslims have lived. Beginning in the twentieth century, Muslims adopted associations in their philanthropic acts to help attain social justice. The examination of Muslim voluntary action has helped explain freedom movements that resulted in independence for many Muslim countries, the fight for civil rights and social justice among Muslim minorities, and the quest for a more just society. The famed twelfth-century theologian, Abu Hamid al-Ghazali (1966) suggests that almsgiving, if done properly, has the dual effect of achieving a more just society, through bridging wealth inequality by requiring those with means to give to those without; and deepening one's devotion and indebtedness to God. The focus on strategy versus injustice is an important difference in notions of Muslim philanthropy. Muslim philanthropy relies on God for impact, as illustrated in an earlier story of the Prophet. However, Muslim philanthropy seeks to further a just society. As Mittermaier (2019, 173) points out through her ethnographic fieldwork, there are real concerns about the structural challenges of an uneven distribution of resources and power. She further reminds us that Muslim donors and volunteers "don't care in the way we might want them to care, but they give continuously ... with profound devotion ... [with] an orientation to God" (2019, 180).

Because of the complex interaction of colonization, state control, and a search for religious identity and definition, in the modern world, Muslims are faced with two competing arguments related to Muslim philanthropy. The first argument considers philanthropy to be a personal matter and rejects state control or influence. Mona Atia (2013, 77) points out this tension between Muslim individuals and the state in Egypt. One clear commonality across anthropological work in Muslim-majority societies is the emphasis and strong embrace of informal philanthropy over formalized philanthropy. In some countries, like Indonesia, this emphasis on informal philanthropy over formal philanthropy is embraced by what scholar Amelia Fauzia calls, "Traditionalist Muslims." Traditionalist Sunni Muslims—a contested category in the field of Islamic studies—are those who accept the four Sunni schools of law and follow the rulings of one particular school (Fauzia 2013, 3). However, there are those, such as Modernists and Revivalists, who wish to bring the state and NGOs into the field of Muslim civic life. Modernists and Revivalists seek guidance directly from the Qur'an and sunna and draw upon multiple schools rather than one of the four Sunni schools of law, sometimes even eschewing affiliation with such schools in total (Fauzia 2013, 4). These are heuristic categories and should not be taken up by scholars and adapted to all Muslim debates about the proper relationship between state and society. Many groups in the Middle East, North Africa, South and Southeast Asia, Europe, and North America do not fit neatly into the dichotomy of Traditionalist vs. Modernist/ Revivalist. However, Fauzia has developed a helpful heuristic for thinking about the different tensions, normative arguments, and debates that Muslims have with each other concerning Muslim philanthropy (2013, 5):

• Those who favor state control over the economic and financial dimensions of faith practice.

- Those who are against interference and institutionalization by the state.
- Those who want to keep philanthropy in the hands of non-state actors but demand mutual support from the state.

As we discussed earlier, these positions are further complicated when we try to fit the Muslim practice of philanthropy within the confines of the Western definition of philanthropy. For example, on March 25, 2010, Dr. Ingrid Mattson delivered the Seventh Annual Thomas H. Lake Lecture to an audience of approximately 120 in- and out-of-state people who came to hear her speak. Among those in attendance were university professors, students, leadership of the Islamic Society of North America, Jewish and Christian clergy, and representatives of multiple Indianapolis-area Muslim congregations (Mattson 2010).

Mattson served as the first female president of the Islamic Society of North America (ISNA) and is a noted Islamic scholar. Mattson argued that zakat was in fact a wealth tax that fell outside the definition of philanthropy. However, she suggests that, in the modern United States, zakat could be used to balance the needs of struggling Muslims. Mattson views the institution of zakat through two lenses: first, through the perspective of a Revivalist who sought to define the practice through the sunna of the Prophet, during which period, zakat was collected by the state; second, through the modern definition of philanthropy (voluntary action for the public good). The fact that zakat is required or that the government may play a role in this act of charity excluded it from the definition of philanthropy. However, both positions are in tension with a large portion of the so-called Muslim world that treats zakat as an act of personal, yet obligatory, charity (Fauzia 2013, 260). As mentioned earlier, Mattson is not alone in this position. Singer and Payton have argued similar positions on zakat. The tension between the role of the state and religious philanthropy is best illustrated through the example of Muslim-American philanthropy due to increased government scrutiny after the terrorist attacks on September 11, 2001. By focusing on philanthropy as defined in the West, Muslim Americans did not address the main threat to Muslim-American philanthropy in a post-9/11 context.

CONCLUSION

Understanding Muslim philanthropy is both constrained and enabled by the fact that Muslims are incredibly diverse. This chapter seeks to aid in understanding Muslim diversity by exploring further the Sunni tradition as one example. However, as we have seen, this exploration is limited at best. Volumes can be devoted to the development of Sunni thought and its various schools, not to mention the many other forms and practices such as khums, a form of obligatory giving for Shi'i Muslims. Each Muslim tradition has a diverse understanding of the practice and theology of Islam. If we consider the hadith that includes smiling, we could potentially propose the following definition of Muslim philanthropy: "intentional choices that seek to further one's relationship with God by advancing the perceived common good." Furthermore, not all schools of religious thought may be aligned on the use of this hadith as the central definer of Islamic practice of philanthropy, and not all Muslims rely on theology to determine their religious identity. A more inclusive definition may be "intentional choices influenced by religious, cultural, or social factors among individuals who identify as Muslims and who seek to advance the perceived common good." Or perhaps we could visualize a diverse group of Muslims through the lens of their localized and individualized embrace of their Muslim identity and how it informs their philanthropic activity.

Western scholars have sought to define philanthropy in a way that makes it difficult for religions, especially non-Euro-American Christian traditions, to have a more comprehensive self-examination of their own charitable and humanitarian acts. It is critical that we interrogate these notions in order to comprehend their limitations toward understanding Muslim philanthropy. Furthermore, the attempt to differentiate charity from philanthropy can increase the exclusion of non-Western and nonreligious acts. Having a definition may be a useful starting point for scholars of philanthropy. However, when examining norms or traditions that fall outside the Western conception of philanthropy, this definition should not inhibit scholars from constantly reevaluating our understanding of philanthropy. Developing a framework to examine philanthropy in a more comprehensive and interdisciplinary manner will help us make the field more vibrant. The lack of best practices, measures of accountability, or management techniques are not the principal challenges to the field of philanthropy. In fact, the field of philanthropic studies has been too content with the legacy of scientific philanthropy to better express impacts. The real danger to our field is the need to quickly define and limit philanthropy. Muslim scholars, practitioners, and policymakers need to explore their own cultural, religious, and historical traditions to develop a constantly evolving definition of philanthropy. For centuries, Muslim philanthropy has lived well beyond the narrow scope of a Western definition.

NOTE

1. This chapter draws upon prior work by author Shariq Siddiqui, including: "Muslim Philanthropy: Living Beyond a Western Definition," *Voluntary Sector Review* (2022): 1–17; "Giving in the Way of God: Muslim Philanthropy in the United States," in *Religious Giving: For Love of God*, edited by D. Smith, 28–47 (Bloomington: Indiana University Press, 2010).

2. Studying Muslim philanthropy through data

Muslims give generously across the globe. Despite the widescale prevalence of charity in Islam, only some studies have attempted to measure it, meaning that scholars and practitioners must be fully aware of its scope and size. Therefore, in this chapter, we examine existing Muslim philanthropy data using international surveys from 2000 to 2021. We compare findings across these data sources to assess how Muslim philanthropy varies worldwide. This study finds several similarities and differences across the Muslim world. We find that Muslims like to donate to individuals rather than institutions and that religion is the primary motivator behind philanthropic giving across most of the Muslim world. However, several sociodemographic factors, such as marital status, wealth, education, and age, affect Muslims' motivation for giving; there are several differences in altruism across the globe, as countries lie differently on a continuum of benevolence. We end with recommendations on how to perceive Muslim philanthropy and on future research needed to explore and compare Muslim giving globally.

OVERVIEW OF THE SOCIAL AND ECONOMIC ISSUES FACED BY THE MUSLIM WORLD

With 1.8 billion adherents, Islam is the second-largest religion in the world after Christianity (Lipka 2017). Approximately 62 percent of the world's Muslims live in Asia, with over 683 million adherents in countries such as Indonesia (the largest Muslim country by population and home to 15.6 percent of the world's Muslims), Pakistan, India, and Bangladesh. About 20 percent of Muslims live in Arab countries. In the Middle East, the non-Arab countries of Turkey and Iran are the largest Muslim-majority countries, and in Africa, Egypt and Nigeria have the most populous Muslim communities (Lipka 2017).

Approximately 70 percent of Muslims live in 47 Muslim-majority countries in Africa and Asia, with substantial minorities across other parts of the world, including India, the United States, the United Kingdom, and France. The proportions of the Muslim population vary significantly, ranging from about 50 percent in five Muslim-majority countries in sub-Saharan Africa (50 percent in Nigeria and Burkina Faso, 51 percent in Eritrea, 52 percent in

Guinea-Bissau, and 53 percent in Chad) to almost 100 percent (no country is truly 100 percent Muslim) in nine Muslim-majority countries (Afghanistan, Mauritania, Oman, Qatar, Somalia, Tunisia, Yemen, Maldives, and Saudi Arabia). Additionally, Muslims form substantial minorities in different parts of the world, including India, Ethiopia, Russia, Tanzania, and France (Siddiqui 2010; Alsultany 2007). Organisation of Islamic Cooperation (OIC) members range from countries reporting close to 99.9 percent Muslim to those reporting only 20 percent Muslim.

Statistical comparisons such as those in the 2020 Human Development Index (HDI) report (United Nations Development Programme 2020) suggest a low level of human development across the Muslim world. Despite its immense wealth, the United Arab Emirates has a value of 0.890 and is 31st on the list, followed by Saudi Arab at 40, with Yemen, Sudan, Afghanistan, and several countries in Africa such as Niger and Chad at the lowest end of the report.

Thus, it is no surprise that poverty issues run rampant across the Muslim world. For example, of the 52 OIC countries, 25 are among the 56 most poverty-stricken countries of sub-Saharan Africa and South Asia. In terms of human development, most Muslim countries fall outside the top 100 countries, which clearly illustrates those countries' severe developmental challenges.

Curbing Inequalities

These countries also face severe economic inequality (Amr, Mogahed, and Marshall, 2008). Curbing those inequalities and injustices in society is central to Islamic observance, which encourages the fair distribution of wealth (S. Khan 2015; Siddiqui 2010). The tradition of Muslim philanthropy dates to the earliest days of the religion, but judging its scale is challenging given the myriad forms of Muslim giving worldwide (Wasif and Prakash 2017).

In general, Muslims are very generous with their donations. According to the best estimates proposed by the United States Agency for International Development (USAID), charitable giving in the Muslim world is between $250 billion and $1 trillion (Alterman, Hunter, and Phillips 2005). Consequently, the Muslim world brings substantial charitable giving to fruition.

Muslims' giving practices are also spontaneous; they wish to give generously but lack interest in partnering or measuring the impact of their donations (Siddiqui 2010). As a result, very few data points exist to document Muslim philanthropy, including global data. Only the Gallup World Poll provides comparative global data that includes three main philanthropy measures: willingness to help a stranger, donating money, and volunteering. The Charities Aid Foundation (CAF 2019) averages these three measures to rank different countries.

The Gallup World Poll conducts a nationally representative survey of individuals in 150 countries, representing more than 99 percent of the world's adult population. It uses randomly selected nationally representative samples. Gallup typically surveys 1,000 individuals in each country using a standardized questionnaire. The Country Data Set Details document displays each country's sample size, month and year of the data collection, mode of interviewing, languages employed, design effect, the margin of error, and details about sample coverage (CAF 2019). These are the most comprehensive comparative data on the determinants of Muslim philanthropy globally. They are a rich source for understanding how other motives, such as sociodemographic status and opinions about the state and other actors, may influence philanthropy across the Muslim world.

However, very little research has documented Muslim philanthropy, and we have little information on the causes Muslims like to pursue and what political beliefs or motives underlie their giving. Also, nothing of the existing literature focuses on what motivates Muslims to give, their causes, and a comparative analysis of how Muslim giving differs by region across the globe and within countries. The lack of data and research in this area emphasizes the importance of tapping into the rich resource stream worth millions of dollars from Muslim faith-based giving (Siddiqui 2010).

As a result, scholars can ask several essential questions, such as the impact of political beliefs and other critical issues on philanthropy. With such information, philanthropic organizations can better target their charitable efforts to raise funds. We also need to determine if these philanthropic gifts are strategically channeled to major needs or what causes they need to be directed to.

Nonprofits and charitable organizations can use such data to improve their lobbying efforts with the government to introduce policies that encourage charitable giving among the populations. Moreover, Muslims are a heterogenous group, divided along ethnic, sect, and socioeconomic demographics. Although there are some wealthy countries, for example, the Gulf countries, others are some of the poorest in the world, including countries in sub-Saharan Africa such as Yemen and Syria (S. Khan and Siddiqui 2017). The following section examines major surveys conducted on Muslim giving.

MAJOR SURVEYS ON MUSLIM GIVING

Currently, no exact estimates are available on how much Muslims give. As mentioned earlier, even the USAID study estimated a broad range of between $250 billion and $1 trillion of Muslim giving (Alterman et al. 2005). Although there are few estimates of overall Muslim giving, several international surveys in Muslim-majority countries have estimated their overall giving. For instance, charitable giving in Pakistan increased from $815 million in 2000 to $2.4

billion in 2014. Similarly, it suggests a wide variation in the zakat potential of different Muslim-majority countries, from $950 million in Egypt to $22 billion in Indonesia.

Very few studies have been conducted worldwide to gauge Muslim giving. It also suggests considerable variations in Muslim giving and variations across time. Moreover, in the case of Turkey, Indonesia, and Pakistan, overall, Muslim giving is on the rise, thus suggesting that, as these countries develop, their citizens are more likely to give money. Also noteworthy is the fact that no, or very few, studies have gauged the size of giving in some of the wealthiest Muslim countries, such as Saudi Arabia, Qatar, and the United Arab Emirates. Gaining a better idea about such countries' giving habits will help policymakers understand overall giving in the Muslim world.

Pakistan

Several surveys in Pakistan have tried to gauge the scope of philanthropy in the country. The first national study in Pakistan by the Aga Khan Foundation estimated giving at $815 million in 2000 (Jadoon and Hasan 2006). Groundbreaking, the survey revealed that religion influenced most of the giving, as 94 percent went toward religious causes. The survey also revealed the informal nature of giving, as most of the giving (65 percent) went directly to individuals instead of organizations.

Latest giving

The Pakistan Centre for Philanthropy (PCP) published a report on giving in 2021, focusing on giving amongst Pakistanis. PCP surveyed during the time of Ramadan. It found that eight out of ten surveyed had been given money over the last year. This giving was lower than the last report (2014) where 98 percent of respondents had reported giving money. On average, they found that an average Pakistani gave Rs 10,000. About 84 percent of individual respondents claim to have given charity in one form or the other during past one year. A relatively lower score of giving is reported for rural respondents (81 percent) than their urban counterparts (86 percent). However, there are no significant variations in giving among provinces in Pakistan.

Motivations for giving

Religion is the most common motivation for giving charity as stated by 67 percent of respondents. Twenty-six percent of respondents wanted to help those that were less fortunate than themselves. On the other hand, 21 percent cited "I believe we need to help/solve social problems" as the reason they give. Eleven percent cited "I care about the cause" as the main reason behind their giving. This finding was confirmed by other previous surveys by the Pakistan

Centre for Philanthropy (2014) that confirmed that religion was the primary motivation behind giving.

The Pakistan Centre for Philanthropy (PCP) had conducted previous surveys in Pakistan on individual giving, including 10,000 individuals, for 2013 and 2014.

Reasons for individual giving as opposed to institutional giving

Informal philanthropy comprised the largest part of giving. The major recipients of charity are poor persons or a family that the respondents know personally (46 percent), and the beggar they come across on the street (44 percent). The lowest score is for organization/institutions as recipients of charitable giving, as only 10 percent of females and 13 percent of males gave to organizations.

While the 2021 PCP survey did not specifically ask what prompted the preference for giving to individuals rather than organizations, the 2014 survey had also conducted focus group discussions centered on the preference. Findings from the focus groups suggest that donors mistrust philanthropic organizations and are hesitant to donate to them. In the focus groups, individuals indicated that they were more likely to contribute to organizations with greater transparency in their work and if the decision-making was local.

The focus group participants also needed to be aware of eligible and trustworthy zakat organizational recipients and the tax exemptions for philanthropic giving. Focus groups furthermore revealed that donors were more willing to donate to organizations whose values aligned closely with local needs. The findings suggest that individuals are less likely to contribute to organizations because of low trust and transparency and a need for more awareness about eligible organizations willing to take their donations.

Turkey

Several surveys have also attempted to gauge the size of philanthropy in Turkey. The first major survey of Turkish charities undertaken in 2004 reported almost $2 billion in total income from charitable contributions. The second major survey was conducted in 2014, followed by the latest one 2019. The Third Sector Foundation of Turkey (TUSEV) conducted these surveys. It estimated that philanthropic giving was $4.2 billion in 2019, double that in 2004. The findings suggest that the overall scope of giving is rising in Turkey.

Turkish survey 2019

Several of the findings in this survey are like those in Pakistan. There was a high level of non-cash philanthropy, with a significant proportion (40 percent) of individuals reporting an informal donation to a relative, neighbor, or other needy individuals. However, different from earlier surveys, this one showed that, increasingly, individuals are more likely to give cash instead of in-kind donations. While the survey did not divide the giving into religious or secular contributions, it did report that zakat (19.5 percent) and sadaqa (18.2 percent) constituted nearly 38 percent of overall giving.

The survey showed that, as in Pakistan, citizens preferred to direct their donations to those in need rather than through an organization. In the case of Turkey, only 12 percent of people reported donating through organizations. Donations to beggars were prevalent, and 40 percent of citizens reported giving money to them. Like Pakistan, one of the prime reasons for not giving more to organizations was a need for more trust in their work. For instance, most Turkish respondents reported that they would be more likely to donate to an organization in the next 12 months if there were more transparency in civil society (55.2 percent), suggesting an acute lack of trust in these organizations' work. Respondents also believed that civil society organizations (CSOs) had limited influence over their activity areas and state policies.

Thus, based on the Turkish survey, individuals are more likely to believe that these organizations are ineffective, in addition to a lack of trust in organizations. Interestingly, they also think that their donations are too small and irregular to give to an organization, which may suggest that these organizations need to increase their outreach to receive small donor grants.

Main motivations for giving
There were several factors behind what motivates people to give. The survey found one interesting similar effect of religious faith in Turkey and Pakistan: in Turkey, individuals were less likely to cite religion (64 percent) as a motivator for charitable giving, whereas, in Pakistan, more than 67 percent of respondents cited religious motivation as the primary reason behind their donations. Social norms also played a large role in individual contributions, as respondents cited these as one of the main reasons for giving (46.6 percent). Trust in organizations was also an important reason for giving (55 percent of respondents cited it as one of the main reasons). Other primary reasons behind donating in the past 12 months were "the desire to help those in distress," "personal fulfillment," and "the importance of the subject of donation."

In addition, the survey asked respondents what would motivate them to contribute in the next 12 months. Their responses indicated that vital factors were "having more money," "being assured of the intended use of the donation," and "higher transparency of CSOs." Thus, the transparency of organizations is an important factor for Turkish donors. Another finding showed that 36.7 percent of respondents said they were likely to give if asked to do so. This finding suggests that philanthropic organizations and individuals may be able to get people to give more if individuals are asked more often for donations.

Egypt

Egypt is a regional power in North Africa, the Middle East, and the Muslim world. It has the second largest economy in Africa, the world's 33rd largest economy by nominal GDP, and the 19th largest by PPP. Historically, Egypt has also been the most prominent Muslim country and claims to be one of the world's oldest and most prosperous civilizations. However, despite its incredible economic potential, the study of Egypt in the context of philanthropy is lacking. Marwa El Daly (2012) conducted the last central mapping of Egyptian generosity. According to Daly, Egyptians donated the equivalent of $950 million (i.e., close to $1 billion) annually, much less than other countries.

Motivations for donations

The Egyptian survey conducted by Daly showed that religious obligations and duties are the main reasons for giving, as in other parts of the world. For instance, many said that meeting their religious duties and getting closer to God was very important (45.8 percent and 37.2 percent, respectively, putting this as their first choice). Social norms also played a prominent role in individuals' decisions to donate (13.3 percent had this as the first choice). Benefitting the poor, helping the government reduce poverty, and public economic and social good were very low on the list of motivations for giving, which may reflect low trust in the government's ability to reduce poverty.

Motivations for philanthropy

As in other parts of the Muslim world, in Egypt most of the philanthropy was directed to individuals instead of institutions. People first helped their relatives (78.6 percent) and then helped people in their neighborhood (36.3 percent). Again, very few individuals said they would donate to organizations, with only 3 percent likely to do so instead of contributing to an individual; 8.9 percent had donating to an organization as their second choice, and 8.7 percent had it as their third preference. Similarly, only 6.4 percent of the respondents agreed they were willing to donate to charity through institutions, while an overwhelming 81.1 percent suggested channeling their charity through individuals.

Respondents were also asked why they did not donate to institutions. Interestingly, in the case of Egypt, the main reason was that individuals preferred giving to their relatives and people close to them. As with the respondents in Turkey, those in Egypt also said their donations needed to be more substantial to be channeled to a nonprofit (26.5 percent). Hence, they did not need an intermediary to channel their donations (26.7 percent).

Many respondents (15 percent) did not direct their religious giving through organizations because they needed to learn about their existence and role (7.5 percent). Only 8.2 percent of respondents said they did not donate to civil rights organizations because they did not trust them, which was lower than in Pakistan and Turkey.

Indonesia

Indonesians are strongly motivated to give to religious causes (Fauzia 2008), and Indonesia had the highest rate of religiously motivated charitable giving globally (98 percent) in 2019. The National Board of Zakat estimated the country's philanthropy at around $22 billion (3.4 percent of GDP) in 2012. In 2019, 98 percent of Indonesians reported that they give charitably, the highest rate by world standards. Indonesia also stands apart in the CAF rating, as it was the Muslim-majority country with the highest rating (10) in 2019. It is also the only country with a top-ten ranking that has risen in rank since 2010.

The Indonesia Family Life Survey involved 12,692 respondents. The survey was unique because it asked respondents separately about their religiously motivated and secularly motivated giving. The average contribution to religious causes was $166, 79 percent of the average donation, whereas secular causes comprised 21 percent. Thus, overall contributions to these causes came to $53.8 billion, higher than any other country.

Una Osili and Çağla Ökten's (2015) survey analysis revealed several interesting findings. For instance, it showed that religion affects giving, with households headed by a Christian being 1.38 times more likely to have given than households headed by a Muslim. Age, education, marital status, and homeownership positively affected total contributions. However, some differences existed in the effect of education on religious and secular donations. Higher education, for example, did not increase the odds of religious giving but did increase secular giving. A junior high school graduate was 1.5 times more likely to give to a secular cause than a primary school graduate. Religiosity also affected giving, as self-reported religiosity increased the amount donated. Finally, household heads with trusting attitudes toward others gave 29 percent more to organizations than those who entirely distrust others.

Motivations for giving
The Indonesian survey did not ask respondents about their motivations for giving. However, we looked at a study on giving behaviors in Indonesia that noted several reasons for giving, including the perception of financial security, perceived importance of religion, the feeling of duty and responsibility to help the needy, desire to make a change, religious concerns, and self-satisfaction from having a significant impact on charitable donations (Awaliah Kasri 2013). The research did not give the percentage of respondents who held these convictions. However, the study did show that all these factors significantly affected the overall giving of respondents.

COMPARATIVE SURVEYS

Several comparative surveys have looked at Muslim philanthropy more globally. For example, a 2012 Pew Research survey included 38,000 Muslims in the following countries: Afghanistan, Albania, Azerbaijan, Bangladesh, Bosnia-Herzegovina, Egypt, Indonesia, Iraq, Jordan, Kazakhstan, Kosovo, Kyrgyzstan, Lebanon, Malaysia, Morocco, Niger, Pakistan, Palestinian Territories, Russia, Tajikistan, Thailand, Tunisia, Turkey, and Uzbekistan (Lipka 2017).

The survey asked respondents if they had paid zakat over the past year. The results showed differences among Muslims' zakat practices, though most paid zakat. In Southeast Asia and South Asia, a median of roughly nine in ten Muslims (93 percent and 89 percent, respectively) said they performed zakat. At least three-quarters of respondents in the Middle East and North Africa (79 percent) and sub-Saharan Africa (77 percent) also said they performed zakat. Furthermore, smaller majorities in Central Asia (69 percent) and Southern and Eastern Europe (56 percent) said they practiced annual almsgiving.

The Pew Research Center (2012) found major differences at the country level across the Muslim world. However, in 36 of the 39 countries surveyed, most Muslims said they engaged in traditional giving of alms; for example, in Southeast Asia, this included nearly all Muslims in Indonesia (98 percent) and more than nine in ten in Malaysia and Thailand (93 percent). Annual almsgiving rates were nearly as high in South Asia, with roughly nine in ten in Afghanistan (91 percent) and Pakistan (89 percent) observing zakat. Fewer in Bangladesh (78 percent) reported giving alms. Morocco stood out among the countries surveyed in the Middle East and North Africa, with 92 percent of Muslims saying they made annual donations to the poor. At least seven in ten in the Palestinian territories (84 percent), Tunisia (81 percent), Iraq (79 percent), Lebanon (78 percent), Jordan (74 percent), and Egypt (70 percent) also said they gave alms annually.

Rates of zakat observance in sub-Saharan Africa ranged from 89 percent in Liberia to 58 percent in Mozambique. In most of the countries surveyed in the region, two-thirds or more of Muslims said they annually donated a percentage of their wealth to charity or the mosque. However, it was less common in post-Soviet states in Central Asia and across Southern and Eastern Europe. Even in those countries, a substantial percentage of Muslims gave zakat. For example, roughly two-thirds or more in Bosnia-Herzegovina (81 percent), Kyrgyzstan (77 percent), Uzbekistan (73 percent), Turkey (72 percent), Kosovo (69 percent), and Tajikistan (66 percent) said they gave alms annually. Substantial minorities in Albania (43 percent), Russia (39 percent), and Kazakhstan (36 percent) did the same.

The survey also asked questions about religiosity and sociodemographic influences. However, the survey did not analyze the impact of these factors on the likelihood of giving zakat. Nevertheless, researchers can use the data in this survey to better understand Muslims' potential to pay zakat and their other religious beliefs and practices, such as mosque attendance; and how the practice of paying zakat may vary by region and sect. However, the survey is limited because it asked respondents only whether they had paid zakat. Thus, it did not provide an estimate on how much zakat or charity they paid. Similarly, it did not ask what specific causes or institutions or individuals received zakat from them.

Arab Barometer

Arab Barometer has examined several Muslim-majority countries, including Algeria, Egypt, Iraq, Jordan, Kuwait, Lebanon, Libya, Morocco, Palestine, Sudan, Tunisia, and Yemen. There have been seven different waves of surveys by Arab Barometer, including surveys of social, political, and economic attitudes and values in the Arab world, which all together included more than 70,000 interviews. The survey asked questions about governance and political affairs, socioeconomic demographics, gender equality, religiosity and politics, and perceptions about religion and foreign countries. The survey also queried individuals about their philanthropic practices. The survey asked individuals if they preferred sadaqa or taxation as the best way to eliminate poverty.

Based on the surveys by Arab Barometer, most MENA regions believe the principle of sadaqa over taxation is the most effective way to help those in need. In 2016 through 2017, six in ten respondents said they would prefer sadaqa as the best way of reducing poverty. In a cross-country comparison, two-thirds of Iraqis, 64 percent of Libyans, and 62 percent of Palestinians and Tunisians said sadaqa is the best way to reduce poverty, compared with 33 percent in Egypt, 27 percent in Yemen, and 20 percent in Morocco. The last survey in 2021 did not ask this question about sadaqa. Thus, this finding suggests substantial variations on how Muslims in the region perceive the importance of sadaqa.

Respondents' ages affected their perception of the importance of sadaqa over taxation; thus, examining differences by age yielded mixed results. Age differences also existed regarding reporting charity. Older generations were more likely to report donating to charity annually throughout the region than younger generations. However, there were some regional differences, as in some parts of the MENA region (Sudan, Kuwait, and Lebanon) no substantial differences existed on the importance of sadaqa over taxation.

Also, a slight gender gap affected the choice of sadaqa. Women across the region consistently voiced a stronger preference for sadaqa than men.

Regarding giving behaviors, in most countries, males were more likely to say they donated in an average month, although women were more likely to do so in Egypt and Algeria. No substantive difference was found in Libya, Morocco, and Lebanon.

The survey showed that, in all countries except Kuwait and Yemen, individuals with higher levels of education gave more to charity in an average month. Additionally, higher-income people in all the countries surveyed were more likely to donate frequently to charity.

When asked whether people were willing to help the poor, even if doing so came at personal cost, almost one-third (31.3 percent) reported that they were happy to do so, although a majority of people (62.2 percent) stated they were willing to be charitable as long as it involved only a small personal cost. Only 2.3 percent of the Arab public said they would not help the poor. There appears to be no difference in giving by gender or age across the region and no variation across major religions, with Muslims and Christians reporting to be equally charitable. The 2021 survey also asked this question, but we could not find any report or analysis that focused on 2021 data, although scholars can analyze this data themselves in the future.

Variations along national lines showed up in the respondents' answers. Palestinians (40 percent), Algerians (38 percent), and Tunisians (37 percent) were most willing to help the poor, even if it involved high costs for themselves. Nearly one-third (33 percent) of Jordanians reported they were happy to help those in need, even if it was expensive. About one-quarter of the Lebanese (27 percent) and Moroccan (26 percent) respondents said they would help the poor at any cost. In Egypt, only two in ten said they would be ready to help, even if it involved high costs for themselves.

Motivations for giving

The survey gives us an idea of the primary motivation for charitable giving. Of course, these reports may vary by social-desirability pressures. Across the region, religion was the primary motivation behind giving, as most people (51 percent) said this was their primary motivation to help. This motivation, however, was followed by desiring not to see people suffer (23 percent), enjoying making people happy (15 percent), and wanting to make the community a better place (7 percent). The survey did not ask questions about the role of social norms in individuals' decisions to donate.

Other Measures

The Global Preference Survey (GPS) is a dataset of time preference, risk preference, positive and negative reciprocity, altruism, and trust from 80,000 people in 76 countries—including from several Muslim countries (Falk et al.

2018). It measures these factors by using one quantitative and one qualitative question relating to donations. The first question asks respondents how much of this money they would donate if they were to unexpectedly receive 1,000 euros. The qualitative items asked how willing respondents would be to give to good causes without expecting anything in return on an 11-point scale.

Higher values indicate the country's average for altruism is above the world average. For instance, while Morocco and Iran are high on the altruism assessment scale, Saudi Arabia and Algeria are low. As with Algeria and Morocco, neighboring countries may vary substantially in their altruism.

Also, several datasets ask questions about giving or zakat in the context of Muslim countries. As an illustration, the 2010 Sub-Saharan Africa Religion Survey examined Botswana, Cameroon, Chad, Congo, Djibouti, Ethiopia, Ghana, Guinea Bissau, Kenya, Liberia, Mali, Mozambique, Nigeria, Rwanda, Senegal, South Africa, and Senegal (Pew 2010). However, no studies have analyzed the results for these datasets so far.

CONCLUSION

After examining and comparing data on Muslim philanthropy in existing international surveys conducted by groups such as the Pew Research Center, the Human Development Index, the Charities Aid Foundation, the Gallup World Poll, and the Institute of Social and Policy Understanding—with a specific focus on the giving practices of respondents in Pakistan, Turkey, Egypt, and Indonesia—we find several similarities and differences across the Muslim world. The results show several differences in altruism and generosity across the globe, as countries lie differently on a continuum of benevolence.

We also find that religiosity is one of the primary drivers of philanthropy across the Muslim world. Additionally, factors like gender and social norms, such as marital status, wealth, education, and age, affect the motivation to give as well as the amount of money given.

Limitations and Future Studies

The data noted in this chapter are based on surveys that asked respondents different questions. For instance, the study on Turkey asked questions about motivations to give that should have been included in the survey of Pakistani respondents. In contrast, the Indonesian poll did not have questions on this topic.

On the other hand, cross-country comparison surveys like those conducted by the Pew Research Center and Gallup are helpful, as they allow us to compare Muslim philanthropy across different geographical areas. However, these surveys are also limited, as they often focused on something other than philanthropy, and their questions were limited. For instance, the Pew survey noted in this chapter asked respondents only whether they had donated zakat over the past year, not the amount of zakat that they had given. Similarly, the Gallup survey asked individuals whether they had given to charity or volunteered over the previous month. While we can ascertain whether individuals gave over the past month, because of the limited questions we need to know what cause the respondents gave to and cannot determine the total amount of their donations.

To better understand how Muslims donate worldwide, future surveys need to include questions related to the amount of money they give and the causes they contribute to. Studies that delve more deeply into questions about motivations and questions on religiosity and sociodemographic factors are needed. Moreover, most of the research on Muslim philanthropy so far has been descriptive in nature. This means, for example, that we can get an idea about overall generosity, but we need to know what factors drive this philanthropy. The only research we found that did so was in Indonesia, where the authors applied multivariate regressions to determine what sociodemographic factors affect charitable giving to various causes. However, as most of the research is descriptive, we cannot do similar analyses across multiple parts of the world. Moreover, it is crucial to perform multivariate regressions on these data to understand better what motivates different Muslims to give to other causes.

3. Zakat in modern America

And establish prayer and give zakāh, and whatever good you put forward for
yourselves—you will find it with Allāh. Indeed Allāh, of what you do, is Seeing.
Qur'an 2:110

Ancient civilizations have bequeathed many philanthropic concepts, practices, and institutions to the modern social order. They showed concern for
the less fortunate, the poor, and the needy by giving time and money, even
forming voluntary organizations to provide such services. Moreover, religious
traditions developed strong mechanisms to encourage giving. For instance,
there is evidence of voluntary associations in the Old Testament (Ross 1974).
This is true for the three largest Abrahamic religions: Islam, Christianity, and
Judaism. Each have an organized mechanism for giving: tithing in Christianity,
tzedakah in Judaism, and zakat in Islam.

These traditions of giving influenced each other. As an illustration, Judaism
encouraged helping the poor through relief and charity. Ancient Jews believed
that their reward for supporting the poor would come directly from God,
unlike Greco-Roman traditions that expected tangible returns directly from
the recipients of their gifts. Christianity and Jesus followed these ideas. For
example, Jesus rejected the Greek practice of limiting home hospitality to
the rich who could reciprocate such favors and instead urged his followers to
pursue the Jewish practice of inviting the poor, even if they could not reciprocate (Loewenberg 1994).

These traditions evolved over time. For instance, despite the influence of
Jewish practices, which did not have such requirements and were more decen-
tralized, the charity administration became more centralized, with a greater
role for Christian bishops. As a result, research suggests that, despite having
similar roots, early Christian philanthropic practices evolved and changed
from their Judaic roots.

Even within Jewish traditions, the practices of giving have evolved. For
instance, over time, major changes in the funding of poor relief occurred
among the Jews of ancient Judea. There was more focus on tax-like obligatory
contributions, mostly voluntary individual donations. In Christian countries,
these contributions eventually became taxes that the government levied, but
Jews and dissenters who could not collect taxes developed another way that
included aspects of both voluntary contributions and nonvoluntary contributions (Loewenberg 1995). Even the contemporary practice of giving among

members of the Jewish diaspora has changed due to the influence of the new institutional environment (Shaul Bar Nissim 2019).

Scholars increasingly understand how these philanthropic practices evolved and how they were influenced by local traditions, resulting in diverse practices. To illustrate, although most Christian denominations rely on the Old and New Testaments for their fundamental tenets, their beliefs vary dramatically (Malley 2004). In general, religious narratives of giving embedded in theological principles are deeply influenced by their social and cultural contexts (Robinson 2013).

Additionally, research suggests that the amount people give through tzedakah or tithing is also influenced by several socioeconomic and demographic factors. Thus, within these religious traditions, there are variables such as income, education, gender, age, religious service attendance, congregational size, and the amount of volunteer time devoted to one's group, as well as changes in income (Bekkers and Schuyt 2008; Hoge and Yang 1994; Eckel and Grossman 2004).

Religiosity also impacts these religious practices. An association with a religious identity affects giving, as people with a strong religious identity are likely to give more (Brinkerhoff 2014). Religious groups such as Mormons who have strict policies about religious giving have higher levels of tithing than religious groups that have weaker requirements, such as the Catholic Church (Gill and Pfaff 2010). Similarly, the amount of time an individual has been practicing a faith tradition affects tithing. For instance, Curtis, Evans, and Cnaan (2015) found that lifelong Mormons were more likely to do tithing than new converts, suggesting that the time of conversion affects the likelihood for tithing. Studies also show a positive relationship between religious commitment and higher donations and tithing (Rooney 2010).

Other factors also influence tithing and acts of tzedakah. Bekkers and Wiepking (2011b) identified a variety of mechanisms that can help explain the relationship between religiosity and philanthropy, including altruism (a real concern for others), psychological benefits (earning one's place in heaven, feeling part of a community), values (the importance of helping others), solicitation (receiving requests for contributions), and reputation (recognition from others).

OVERVIEW

Zakat and sadaqa are key Islamic philanthropic traditions. Zakat, the third of five pillars of the Islamic faith, is an obligatory act of giving. Sadaqa is voluntary giving beyond the minimum threshold of zakat. Sadaqa can take the form of money, action, or abstaining from action; the intention behind the action is what constitutes the act as charitable. While there is no prescribed time for giving zakat or sadaqa, many Muslims fulfill charitable obligations during the holy month of Ramadan when acts of charity are emphasized.

Another form of zakat giving in Islam is zakat al-fitr. This is a form of zakat because it is mandatory, meaning the amount and the manner in which it can be donated is prescribed by God and has been elaborated on by Muslim legal scholars for centuries. Zakat al-fitr is donated by Muslims at the end of the holy month of Ramadan. During the lunar month of Ramadan, Muslims fast from dusk to dawn, engage in additional nighttime prayers, and donate to charity. The fast includes no food, drink, or intimate physical contact. Zakat al-fitr is donated at the end of Ramadan before the ritual prayer on Eid al-fitr to celebrate a month of fasting. This form of zakat is mandated to assist those who do not have enough food to celebrate Eid al-fitr. The amount varies depending on the geographic region of the world and the cost of food. In 2021 in Indianapolis, Indiana, zakat al-fitr was calculated as $12 for every member of one's household, including children ("What Is Zakat Al-Fitr, the Special Ramadan Zakat?" n.d.; "How Is Zakat Al-Fitrah Calculated?" 2022).

Research on zakat has frequently focused on religious texts and historical practices to understand how Muslims perceive zakat. However, there has been little research on contemporary Muslim perceptions of zakat and almost no research on estimating the amount of zakat given by US Muslims. Zakat is thought to be a resource for resolving socioeconomic problems, both in Muslim-majority societies and across the globe. However, we need to better understand how and what causes people to give zakat and where they give it, as well as how giving practices differ across varying socioeconomic demographics. With this in mind, we discuss several topics in this chapter. First, we examine certain important scholarly debates related to zakat. Second, we assess how Muslims practice zakat through an original survey of Muslims. By better understanding the major scholarly debates and who gives zakat, how much, and the channels through which they give zakat, we can better recognize and generate policies that can help Muslims fulfill their religious obligations.

In our study, we found that Muslims give zakat generously. Based on our estimated calculation, we found that in 2021 Muslims gave an estimated $1.8 million in zakat. We also found that Muslims in the United States are more likely to conceive of zakat as an act of philanthropy or charity rather than as a tax imposed by religious authorities. These findings show that while there is no debate among Muslim scholars concerning whether giving zakat as stipulated in the Qur'an is an obligatory act, Muslims are generally divided about whether they think of zakat as an act of charity or as something more akin to a tax. Moreover, we find that Muslims give zakat through various avenues.

We found that Muslims use a variety of disbursement mechanisms to give zakat, including formal nonprofits, remittances to various governments that collect zakat, and informal means such as giving directly to individuals or via remittances sent to relatives living abroad. In our study, we did not ask which governments zakat was sent to; however, numerous Muslim-majority countries have zakat collection mechanisms through which individuals can send zakat as remittances. The largest segment of zakat money is disbursed to international nonprofit organizations (NPOs) (25.3 percent), followed by zakat giving to the government (21.7 percent) and domestic NPOs (18.3 percent). Our findings are unique because they show that nearly one in five dollars of US Muslims' zakat money goes to domestic causes in the United States. Our findings also show that a substantial amount of zakat is still being given through informal methods (14.7 percent for giving in person, giving to relatives, etc.) and through remittances (12.7 percent).

CONTEMPORARY DEBATES ON ZAKAT

Zakat practices are part of the Muslim tradition, just as tzedakah and tithing are part of the other Abrahamic traditions. Zakat, or *zakāh* in Arabic, is an act of "financial worship" incumbent on Muslims, stipulated explicitly in the Qur'an, and elaborated on in detail in traditions of Islamic jurisprudence (Benthall 1999). As noted earlier, it is one of the five pillars of Islamic belief and practice, following the profession of God's unity and daily prayers. The verb *zakāh* means "to increase" and "to purify." It "conveys the sense of a payment due on property to purify it and, hence, cause it to be blessed and multiply" (Bashear 1993, 112; Zysow 2012). Zakat functions as an "alms-tax" by which Muslims give a portion of their surplus wealth in the name of God to support those in need, namely the poor. Muslims can deliver zakat directly or through intermediaries such as the state, the mosque, or, increasingly, via institutional actors like Muslim foundations, nonprofits, and humanitarian relief organizations (Henig 2019; Schaeublin 2019; Abraham 2018).

A major concern of scholars and Muslim communities today is zakat eligibility—who can receive it and to what causes it can be given. Qur'an 9:60 details eight categories of those who are eligible to receive zakat:

> Zakāh expenditures are only for the poor and for the needy and for those employed for it and for bringing hearts together [for Islām] and for freeing captives [or slaves] and for those in debt and for the cause of Allāh and for the [stranded] traveler—an obligation [imposed] by Allāh. And Allāh is Knowing and Wise.

Like the traditions discussed earlier in the chapter, zakat practices are evolving. Because religious traditions are not static entities, Muslims debate what these categories mean when they give zakat. While the Qur'an clearly states the several types of recipients, applying these categories to contemporary realities means that Muslims must interpret them in their daily lives. The renowned scholar Shaykh Yusuf al-Qaradawi said:

> As for zakah, it is not purely worshiping, for, in addition to being worship it is a defined right of the poor, an established tax, and an ingredient of the social and economic system of the society. The reasons for enacting zakah are, in general, known and clear. (Qaradawi 2020a, xxxii)

In addition to zakat eligibility, the question of "zakatability" is also significant— on what forms of wealth do Muslims owe zakat, and how is it calculated? The rate of zakat today is estimated at 2.5 percent of surplus wealth above the necessary minimum threshold (or nisab). Determining the amount of zakat owed can be confusing, given the range of accounts, assets, and financial instruments available to people today. Determining zakatability involves careful consideration by scholars and experts who engage in acts of interpretation to translate and apply categories found in Islamic legal texts (such as livestock or wealth held in gold) to conditions of modern banking, finance, and wealth (Latief 2014). These traditions have changed and evolved over time as well.

For example, Muslim institutions have adopted modern technologies to make it easier for Muslims to fulfill their zakat obligations. Today, Muslim organizations in the United States and elsewhere use zakat calculators to determine what an individual owes. For example, Islamic Relief USA, a Muslim humanitarian relief and development organization, collects and distributes zakat; on their website, they stipulate: "Zakat is liable on gold, silver, cash, savings, investments, rent income, business merchandise and profits, shares, securities, and bonds. Zakat is not paid on wealth used for debt repayment of living expenses such as clothing, food, housing, transportation, education, etc." ("Online Zakat Calculator" n.d.). This statement provides a general picture of zakat, but the details are more complicated. For example, there is debate among Muslim scholars about when and how zakat should be paid on retirement accounts. While the categories of who can receive zakat are fairly unambiguous, determining zakatability has proven to be a more contentious issue, given the complications of modern financial life.

Historically, Muslims have debated issues related to zakat, and these debates have continued as Muslims have moved to different parts of the world, lived in majority and minority contexts, and faced different challenges. Timur Kuran (2003) argues that there never has been consensus on how zakat should be paid or collected, and that during the rule of the first few caliphs of Islam following the death of the Prophet, the ways in which zakat was collected were dissimilar.

Singer argues that zakat is misunderstood as philanthropy, as it is not voluntary nor benevolent. However, she concedes that historically there is little evidence that zakat was paid or apportioned by any premodern polity (Singer 2018, 4).

While scholars such as Amy Singer and Ingrid Mattson dispute that zakat is charity as opposed to a tax, the consensus among Muslims is that it is a form of charity that has been institutionalized into the Islamic faith (Ba-Yunus and Kone 2006, 15). Despite significant attempts in countries such as Pakistan, Saudi Arabia, and Malaysia, very few contemporary Muslim-majority nations have centralized systems where state bodies collect zakat (Kuran 2003, 275). Some argue that this is due mainly to the failure of the state to institutionalize zakat and the lack of trust within the state. While in the past, Muslims might have been held accountable for their nonpayment of zakat, scholars note that today most Muslims do not pay zakat through the government and in fact use it to further their charitable interests (McChesney 1995, 7). Abraham (2018) argues that Muslims have long practiced zakat as an informal act and see it as a companion to ritual prayer. Rashid et al. (2017, 163) argue that is it an individual Muslim's obligation to pay zakat and to develop a system to distribute it. There is clearly disagreement among scholars as well as the larger Muslim public about whether zakat is an obligation akin to a tax or whether it falls under the modern concept of charity.

A robust discussion continues today among Muslims about the application of zakat to current circumstances. In his seminal work, *Fiqh al-Zakah: A Comparative Study*, Dr. Yusuf al-Qaradawi (2020a; 2020b) detailed a comprehensive analysis of varying opinions about who should pay zakat, what assets are subject to zakat, and how recipients are defined. Qaradawi spoke, as follows, to Muslim jurists about this historical debate, pointing to the robust discussions in the relevant theological and legal literature from the time of the earliest Muslim communities to the present:

> While comparing different views of the Islamic [Sunni] schools I did not limit myself to the four famous schools, for this might be unjust to other schools and opinions in Islamic jurisprudence. Since there are views expressed by scholars among the Companions, the Followers, and later generations, these views should not be neglected or disregarded. (2020a, xxviii)

One debate, perhaps the most significant one, concerns who is responsible for the collection of zakat. For example, certain Muslim-majority countries have a state mechanism to collect zakat. To illustrate, Powell (2009) noted that the following countries maintain some form of "centralized zakat collection," often pairing government agencies with organizations or by contracting with them, including those in Bangladesh, Bahrain, Egypt, Indonesia, Iran, Jordan, Kuwait, Lebanon, Qatar, Oman, and the United Arab Emirates (Powell 2009, 60). Powell stated that other countries, such as Libya, Malaysia, Pakistan,

Saudi Arabia, Sudan, and Yemen, have legal statues mandating the collection of zakat through government agencies (Powell 2009, 66); and that the countries that do collect zakat have different approaches. For example, Indonesia collects zakat but has a semiautonomous system of authorized organizations that can collect zakat (Powell 2009, 65–6). Alternatively, Pakistan has a centralized and mandatory zakat collection system.

In the non-Muslim-majority context, the consensus among Islamic scholars is that individuals are responsible for paying zakat. Zakat can be paid informally through individuals giving directly to others and formally through institutions that collect and distribute zakat, such as the Zakat Foundation of America, Islamic Relief USA, and the National Zakat Foundation in the United Kingdom, Canada, and Australia, among others. However, nonreligious international relief organizations such as the United Nations High Commissioner for Refugees (UNHCR) and Save the Children have also begun collecting zakat. Importantly, and perhaps most interestingly, the UNHCR has started collecting fatwas (i.e., professional opinions from Islamic scholars and organizations, authorizing the collection and distribution of zakat funds under specific conditions). This practice is not without controversy due to normative concerns about the diffuse nature of decision making in such institutions, questions of accountability and transparency in using zakat funds, and issues relating to various Islamic rules for zakat (Wahb 2023, 19). This issue has created situations in which most non-Muslims or avowedly secular organizations must seek answers to normative theological-legal questions. An indirect consequence of this practice is that these organizations then promote or, at a minimum, accept certain normative positions in Islamic thought that may differ across Islamic schools of interpretation and practice. For example, Save the Children states that it uses "no more than 12.5 percent" for administrative expenses ("Zakat Policy and FAQs" n.d.). They have chosen to adhere to the Shafi'i school's limitation of 12.5 percent of funding to be used for zakat collection. This has, not surprisingly, created some discussion on whether a non-Muslim institution (or government) can collect and distribute zakat. Save the Children has received a religious ruling (fatwa) from Shaykh Haytham Tamim of the UK-based Shariah Solutions, declaring that their zakat policy and its uses are certified as being Shari'a-compliant, which they display on their website. As a further explanation, they state ("Zakat Policy and FAQs" n.d.):

> We have developed a Zakat policy to allow our potential donors to feel confident that donations to Save the Children's Zakat Fund will be used to support our vital work in a number of predominantly Muslim and Muslim-majority countries and communities, in accordance with the principles of Shariah.

Also, the National Zakat Foundation states: "The majority of scholars hold the opinion that zakat is to be both paid and received by Muslims. Other forms of charity such as Sadaqah can be given to Muslims and/or non-Muslims alike" ("Who Can Zakat Not Be Given To?" n.d.).

In the Muslim-minority context, there is also a debate on whether zakat should be given locally or globally. For example, in the United Kingdom, the National Zakat Foundation argues that zakat should be distributed in the local community. Another British charity, Islamic Relief UK, has zakat projects that can be given to support causes inside the United Kingdom as well as overseas. Similarly, in the United States, ICNA Relief raises funds to combat domestic poverty relief and does not take the position that zakat cannot be paid for global causes but encourages Muslims to give zakat locally. The Council of Islamic Organizations of Greater Chicago has established Zakat Chicago to raise and distribute money locally in the city. It does not take the position that zakat cannot be paid globally, but argues it is the preferred way:

> One of the uniqueness of Zakat Chicago is that it operates under the principle of "Local Collection and Local Distribution." It is most preferred to give Zakat locally and a normative tradition demonstrates this since the early days of Islam. The Holy Prophet, his companions and followers of his time and even after used to collect and distribute Zakat locally. Imran bin Husain (may ALLAH be pleased with him), a Companion, was appointed as a zakat collector at the time of the Umayyads. When he returned from his mission, he was asked, "Where is the money?" Imran said, "Did you send me to bring you money? I collected it the same way we used to at the time of the Messenger of God and distributed it the same way we used to" (Sunan Abu Dawud). Zakat Chicago empowers local community, distributes Zakat locally and sponsors and funds local projects like Believer Bailout, Mental Health Counselling and campaigns like Education, Fighting Hunger, Emergency Cash Assistance, Refugee Assistance and New Muslim Support. ("Zakat Chicago—CIOGC" n.d.)

Yousef Aly Wahb (2023) argues that despite the reluctance of American-diaspora Muslims wanting to give zakat overseas (or their original homes), there is ample evidence (including later in this chapter) that this is an important feature of Muslim-American zakat practices. He suggests, "globalization and diaspora reshape modern Muslims' definitions of a community and, therefore, their religious commitments" (2023, 5).

Other important conversations concern whether non-Muslims are eligible for zakat. Wahb assumes that non-Muslims are not eligible for zakat and suggests that Muslim-American domestic support for poverty alleviation (which includes non-Muslims) is "unlikely to be zakah, since the identified recipients of these efforts are largely non-Muslim" (2023, 5). He also suggests that Muslim-American nonprofit institutions are suffering from "definitional manipulation" in at least three categories. He argues that the Qur'anic categories of zakat's eligible expenditures found in Chapter 9, Verse 60—such as "for the cause of Allah," "those whose hearts are to be reconciled," and "those employed to collect it"—are being broadly interpreted and applied in the contemporary context in ways that are questionable to some legal scholars. However, this reinterpretation is not limited only to a Muslim minority context, as many Muslim-majority societies have engaged in centuries-long internal discussion and debate about the application of theological and legal categories to new social, political, and economic formations introduced during the colonial period, during which many Muslims lived under and were subjected to imperial projects of societal transformation by European empires (Asad 1992; Fauzia 2013; Powers 1989; Scott 1999; 2004). Samiul Hasan (2015, 133) illustrates how the Bait al-Mal, the treasury of the Islamic Council of Malaysia, has sought to understand what these categories mean in the contemporary Malaysian context. Like Muslim Americans, Malaysian interpretations have also sought to examine zakat categories to solve contemporary issues and have interpreted these categories similarly.

Wahb's (2023) critique of contemporary zakat interpretation assumes that this practice must be limited to a traditional Islamic interpretation (going back a few hundred years) for how it can be extended. However, Muslim-American practices (by organizations and donors) suggest a more contemporary understanding of what zakat may mean in daily practices in localized contexts. In some cases, this lived understanding has been endorsed by globally recognized Islamic public scholars such as the Qaradawi, Fiqh Council of North America, among others. For example, Islamic Relief USA has adopted the zakat policy of Islamic Relief Worldwide (IR). IR has established an external Zakat Advisory Board consisting of Sheikh Abdullah al-Judai, Mufti Abdul Qadir Barkatulla, and Sheikh Mohammad Akram Nadwi. In addition, IR USA has added Shaikh Muzammil Siddiqi, Shaikh Zulfiqar Ali Shah, Shaikh Mohamed Moussa, and Shaikh Saad Elgedwy to their US-based advisory board ("Our Scholars" n.d.). The crowdfunding site, *LaunchGood*, asked Shaykh Joe Bradford and Shaykh Yaser Birjas to compile its zakat policy and hired Shaykh Aarij Anwer as Zakat Program Manager ("Zakat Policy" n.d.). All these scholars are well known in their geographical context and bring legitimacy and guidance to these institutions on a complicated (and debated) subject. Islamic Relief does not accept zakat funds to reconcile hearts: "As a humanitarian agency we do not engage in any proselytization activity. As such, IR does not undertake zakat activities under the category of mu'allafati quloobuhum [sp]." However, it has (like the Malaysian example) sought to understand and redefine the remaining categories that fit a contemporary context.

There are further discussions about how to reinterpret some other injunctions according to current circumstances. For instance, one zakat category relates to freeing slaves. However, today it is reinterpreted in multiple ways, including helping people who are incarcerated or at risk of being incarcerated.

As an illustration, the Muslim nonprofit organization Believers Bailout (BBO) advocates against the modern industrial prison complex and provides bail funds for pre-incarceration. It reinterpreted the freeing of slaves to include those who are incarcerated. Its home page offers this invitation: "Donate your Zakat and join the movement to end incarceration" (Believers Bail Out n.d.a.). BBO states:

> Zakat, one of the central tenets of Islam, is an annual tax on wealth. The Qur'an (9:60) specifies eight uses for zakat, including helping the poor and the needy and for the freeing of slaves or captives. People being held in pretrial incarceration because they cannot afford bail qualify for zakat. By paying their bail and freeing them to address the charges against them, Believers Bail Out restores the presumption of innocence. It is in our capacity and our duty as Muslims to be a part of ending this unjust bail system that criminalizes poverty and is inherently racist in nature. BBO follows the zakat eligibility and distribution processes outlined by the Tayba Foundation, which also serves incarcerated Muslims.
>
> The use of zakat does not go towards the everyday operations of Believers Bail Out. Zakat monies are used for bond and related fees and post-release support. We firmly believe that based on our understandings of the modern American criminal punishment system that Muslims held in pre-trial and immigration incarceration are captive and held in bondage (fi al-riqab 9:60) and can thus be freed (fakku raqabatin 90:13). At the same time, all of our bailees also qualify for zakat based on their statuses as poor and in-need. (al-fuqaraa wal masakin 9:60) (Believers Bail Out n.d.b)

The Tayba Foundation (Tayba) also works on evidence-based prisoner reentry programs. The programs work with prisoners prior to parole to establish a relationship with case management teams. The Foundation also offers mentoring, training, and case management programs to help eliminate recidivism. Both BBO and Tayba disagree with IR's policy on whether Muslim organizations can use zakat for operations ("Zakat Policy" n.d.). Tayba sought to develop a zakat policy that took the most conservative view from the four schools of Sunni Islam and had their policy reviewed and approved by religious scholars. Tayba requires that students in their program make Tayba the agent (wakil) so that they can accept zakat on behalf of those students. Unlike other Muslim-American nonprofit institutions that do not require this direct connection between the zakat donated and the recipient, Tayba seeks to follow a stricter interpretation of zakat use.

The Assembly of Muslim Jurists of America (AMJA) issued a religious ruling (fatwa) that articulates its position about the use of zakat in the United States ("Zakat-Eligibility of Research-Based Organizations" 2019). Specifically, on the issue of "for the cause of Allah," one member of their committee stated:

> However, some past scholars believed much can fall under the term "and for the cause of Allah," and many contemporary scholars believe it includes protecting the

interests of Islam and the Muslims, da'wah, intellectual efforts, and any related projects that promote them. This was also the conclusion reached by the Islamic Fiqh Council in their 8th conference. Therefore, if the work done by this organization and others like it, which includes gathering detailed and beneficial information concerning Muslims and making them available to those involved in da'wah, [and to] think tanks and policy makers, serves those objectives, then it is eligible to receive Zakat—according to this opinion. In conclusion, AMJA would like to remind all organizations which receive Zakat and [that] benefit from charity of the importance of attentively adhering to the parameters set by the Shariah on receiving and spending Zakat [is] in the correct fashion. (El Haj 2021)

Similarly, the Council on American–Islamic Relations (CAIR) has worked with Dr. Muzammil Siddiqi and Sheikh Ahmad Kutty to develop its position on zakat, stating:

Numerous Muslim scholars have concluded that Zakat is payable to organizations that exist to serve the Muslim community by protecting their rights. This is based on the conclusion that the work done by CAIR (and other such Muslim organizations) can be classified as fi-sabilillah, which is one of the eight categories of Zakat recipients detailed in the Quran (Chapter 9, Verse 60). In addition, CAIR works to help fulfill the Muslim American community's communal obligation (fard kifayah) to protect the right to practice Islam and defend people experiencing unjust oppression. ("Why CAIR Qualifies for Zakat" n.d.)

This section shows that, to meet the needs of the current times, robust debates are taking place in Muslim circles and among scholars and nonprofits in terms of reinterpreting zakat injunctions, including zakat eligibility and the causes that zakat giving can support. These findings suggest that like other faiths, Muslims are constantly trying to better understand how to interpret and reinterpret zakat practices.

METHODS USED IN THE STUDY

This section focuses on the practice of zakat among Muslims in the United States. Our results on Muslim philanthropic practices come from a self-administered web survey on zakat conducted by SSRS for the Indiana University Lilly Family School of Philanthropy. The larger study, of which these findings are a part, surveyed the opinions of Muslims and the general population regarding faith customs, donation practices and attitudes, volunteer work, remittances, tolerance, and diversity. SSRS's survey was conducted from January 25 through February 15, 2022, and comprised 2,010 adult respondents (age 18 and older), including 1,006 Muslim respondents and 1,004 general population respondents. SSRS reached eligible respondents via a nonprobability web panel sample. We restricted questions about zakat and khums to the Muslim sample.

Zakat Findings

As mentioned earlier, our study suggests that Muslims gave approximately $1.8 billion in zakat in 2021. On average, Muslims gave $1,070 in 2021. However, there were differences in the overall zakat giving among Muslims.

Zakat giving by race

The findings showed that, on average, Caucasian Muslims in the United States gave the most in zakat monies ($3,732), followed by Muslims in Asia ($1,089). On average, Arabs and African Americans gave lower amounts of zakat ($569 and $420, respectively), followed by people belonging to mixed ethnicities. In the survey, we asked the participants to self-identify which racial group they belonged to, and we provided the same categories employed by the US Census Bureau.

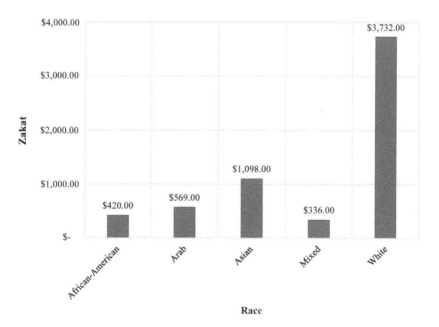

Figure 3.1   Zakat giving by ethnicity

Zakat giving by gender
Similarly, there were gender differences in zakat giving. Males, on average, gave nearly six times ($3,313) more zakat than females ($471). This finding supports those reported in Muslim American Giving 2021 (Siddiqui and Wasif 2021).

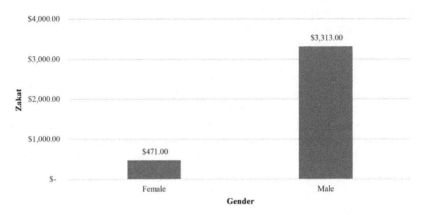

Figure 3.2   Zakat giving by gender

Zakat giving by age
Overall, in terms of zakat giving, individuals aged 40 to 49 gave the most zakat ($2,560), followed by individuals age 18 to 29 ($2,298), which preceded individuals from the 30 to 39 age bracket, the 65 and older age bracket, and the 50 to 54 age bracket. Interestingly, individuals in the 50 to 54 age bracket gave the least zakat on average.

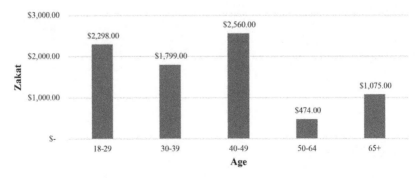

Figure 3.3   Zakat giving by age

Perceptions of Zakat

Research on zakat has frequently focused on religious texts or historical practices to understand how Muslims perceive zakat. However, there has been little research on contemporary Muslim perceptions of zakat and almost no research on Muslim-American perceptions. Therefore, this is one of the first surveys to delve into individual Muslim-Americans' perceptions of zakat, what it means to them, and how they give it.

As stated earlier, zakat is an obligatory act of financial worship with socio-economic effects. According to Muslim scholars and historians, one of zakat's essential purposes has been eliminating poverty and unifying Muslims from different classes. While the purpose of zakat is largely uncontested, historians and anthropologists have debated whether we can understand zakat as an act of philanthropy, a charitable act of worship, or a tax. Since it is not a voluntary, extemporaneous act of giving, scholars often consider it more than an act of philanthropy, as many contemporary Western definitions define it (Richardson 2004). Since it is obligatory, many have suggested that it is similar to a tax mandated by God on the believing person.

This survey asked respondents their opinions of zakat (whether they think of zakat as philanthropy, charity, or tax) on a scale of 1–5. Overall, we found that, on average, individuals are more likely to perceive zakat as an act of charity (mean 4.2) than philanthropy (mean 3.6). Only a small percentage of individuals consider zakat a tax (mean 2.9). These findings evoke new questions about the distinction between charity and philanthropy in Muslim-American communities and how Muslims currently translate religious practices into the dominant terms used to describe acts of beneficence or charitable giving in the United States.

We found that Muslims are significantly more likely to consider zakat as an act of philanthropy than a tax ($p < 0.05$) and as an act of charity rather than a tax ($p < 0.05$). These findings suggest that individuals are more likely to consider zakat as an act of philanthropy than a tax imposed on them.

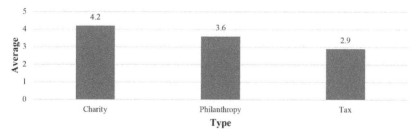

Figure 3.4   Perceptions of zakat

Zakat Distribution

We found that the largest portion of zakat was distributed formally. The largest segment of zakat is disbursed to international NPOs (25.3 percent), followed by zakat giving to the government (21.7 percent) and domestic NPOs (18.3 percent). While we did not ask about which governments zakat was sent to, numerous Muslim-majority countries have a zakat collection mechanism through which individuals can send zakat via remittances. Our findings also show that a substantial amount of zakat is still given through informal methods (14.7 percent for giving in person, giving to relatives, etc.) and through remittances (12.7 percent). These findings suggest that while most of the zakat is distributed formally, nearly a quarter of zakat is distributed informally.

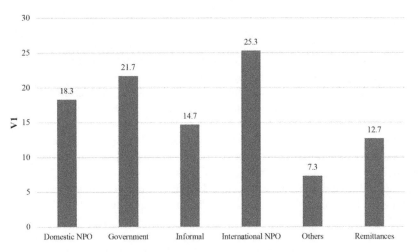

Figure 3.5   Zakat distribution mechanisms

RESULTS SUMMARY

Overall, we found that Muslims are very generous with their zakat practices. Our survey also found that there are considerable racial, gender, and age differences, which are manifested by who gives zakat and how much they can give. The results also indicate a significant higher level of zakat given by self-identified Muslim men, compared with Muslim women. The reason for such gendered differences in zakat giving was not directly explored in this survey, but studies conducted by the Women's Philanthropy Institute at the Lilly Family School of Philanthropy have shown the effects of gender differences on individual and household giving practices. Future studies are needed to explore zakat donation behaviors in more detail from the perspective of gender.

Moreover, Muslims give zakat in diverse ways. Interestingly, while a large segment of zakat is provided either through nonprofits or other institutional means, a substantial proportion is still given informally, either through remittances or in person.

CONCLUSION

This chapter seeks to clarify the Islamic practice of zakat within a contemporary context. We do so because zakat is one of the five pillars of Islam and is an obligatory practice that requires eligible Muslims to give 2.5 percent of their surplus wealth to eight specific (but broadly defined) purposes. We find that Muslims are highly diverse when it comes to their geographic location, ethnic or racial demographics, and theological beliefs. As it is difficult to understand religious practices like zakat in this context, we included theological debates, which we illustrated by using Muslim-Americans' (who themselves are highly diverse with no one ethnic group being a majority) data on zakat. We also shared how these various theological debates play out in Muslim-American nonprofit organizations as well as global non-Muslim nonprofit organizations that seek to raise zakat funds for their work within Muslim-majority contexts.

In addition, we addressed debates on whether the practice of zakat is philanthropy or taxation. We argue that while zakat is a religious obligation, it has been treated as a tax and as an individual philanthropic practice.

The diverse practices of Muslims and Muslim institutions when it comes to zakat suggests that they are seeking to find ways to engage with scholars on the best way to practice zakat in the contemporary context. Traditionally, Muslims have relied on the practice of ijtihad to help them interpret Islamic theological practices in this context. However, the diversity of Muslims, their distrust of institutions, and the availability of scholarly knowledge may be leading us to a place where Muslims are engaged in "lived ijtihad." In essence, they are finding scholars who align with their worldviews, reflect upon those scholarly teachings, and then make a personal determination on how they should practice zakat. Similarly, Muslim nonprofit institutions are reaching out to scholars that their constituencies trust for help in determining the appropriate zakat policy in a contemporary context.

4. Beyond religious texts: discussion of zakat on social media

Despite charity being such a crucial part of Muslim societies, the mainstream media and academia have little understanding of Muslim philanthropy. Few studies exist that document Muslim philanthropy and its motivations and causes. Among those that have conducted surveys, most have underestimated the scope and size of Muslim philanthropy (Siddiqui 2010).

To better understand Muslim philanthropy, we need to determine its effectiveness in alleviating poverty and inequality. In this regard, zakat comes to mind, as it plays an essential role in Muslim philanthropy. However, much of the existing literature on zakat focuses mainly on religious texts, such as the Qur'an and scholars and religious leaders' commentaries about its content (Adachi 2018; Siddiqui 2010).

Even less researched, and thus less understood, is how average Muslims understand the practice of zakat in their everyday lives. In addition, it is important to examine how social media affects the everyday lives of Muslims. As the Arab Spring events in the early 2010s demonstrated, social media can play a crucial role in creating new and dissenting voices and collective action (Hussain and Howard 2013) in the Muslim world and elsewhere.

In this chapter, after a general discussion on the importance of social media and how it is influencing society's beliefs and culture, we discuss how social media has also become an important tool for individuals to both form and share their opinions about their society. We then take a careful look at some recent tweets (tweeted in 2018 through 2019), with a specific focus on zakat and related social comments. In these tweets, Muslim Twitter users (as well as non-Muslims) state their thoughts about zakat to scholars, to charities, and to the invisible audience on social media. Through the use of these tweets, we show how different people define zakat and explore what prompts their various perspectives.

We briefly discuss how such views of zakat can influence our understanding of philanthropy in the Muslim world. Overall, we find that Muslims discuss zakat in both traditional and instrumental frames. While they discuss the moral and religious obligation of zakat and solicit religious scholars' opinions about it, they are also keenly aware of its potential in removing human misery.

Additionally, social media users express concerns about corruption in zakat and that some zakat charity money is funding terrorism.

THE ROLE OF SOCIAL MEDIA IN THE MUSLIM WORLD

The media often portrays Muslims as a marginalized and vulnerable group in imminent need of Western aid (Lajevardi 2019; Wasif 2021). Moreover, because the media routinely associates poverty with terrorism (especially, its concern over terrorist exploitation of Muslim charities), it considers Western aid and charity as critical in the Muslim world to reduce radical violence (E. Berman 2009). On the other hand, the media generally views humanitarianism in Muslim societies through the lens of terrorism and generally ignores Muslim philanthropy altogether (Bano 2012; McClure 2009). Even when the media discusses Muslim philanthropy, it primarily focuses on religious texts and scholarly opinions about philanthropy. As a result, it largely ignores expressions and understandings of charity common among Muslims (Siddiqui 2010).

Therefore, to get a better sense of Muslim philanthropy, we need to understand discourse about philanthropic practices among ordinary Muslims. From the Foucauldian perspective, this discourse can be the instrument and effect of power, a point of resistance, and a starting point for an opposing strategy (Foucault 1995). Social media has enabled us to better understand some of these everyday discourses. With the development of social media, subordinate groups can also voice their opinions more prominently. In the Muslim world, this discourse is playing a crucial role in forming opinions about philanthropy.

Impact of Social Media

Social media and online channels strongly affect people's opinions about philanthropy and inform them about philanthropic causes. For example, in a recent survey, half the respondents agreed that they learned about causes through their use of social media. Nonprofits have embraced social media and use it to expand their outreach to multiple audiences (D. A. Campbell, Lambright, and Wells 2014; Maxwell and Carboni 2016). An emerging body of literature is exploring how nonprofits utilize social media to communicate and engage with stakeholders (Guo 2007; Lovejoy and Saxton 2012; Maxwell and Carboni 2016; Scurlock, Dolsak, and Prakash 2020; Xu and Saxton 2019).

Research on social media and nonprofits has focused on three distinct phases. The first phase focuses on social media adoption in the nonprofit sector (Campbell et al. 2014) and on how nonprofits use social media for their strategic purposes (Guo and Saxton 2014; Jung and Valero 2016; Lai, Bing, and Chen-Chao 2017), for example for fundraising. The third and most recent (and, perhaps, currently most important) stream of nonprofit research focuses on the offline impact of social media on nonprofit operations by looking at the ability of nonprofits to market their activities, maintain relevance, and raise social awareness among their communities (Campbell et al. 2014; Eimhjellen 2014; Farrow and Yuan 2011; Guo and Saxton 2020; Xu and Saxton 2019).

As noted, the second phase targets social media factors such as fundraising. Related literature examines the link between social media usage and fundraising success (Bhati and McDonnell 2020; Castillo, Petrie, and Wardell 2014; Saxton and Wang 2014). Research suggests that social media can help nonprofits and individuals in fundraising. As an illustration, a 24-hour campaign called "#GivingTuesday" raised more than \$168 million in charitable donations worldwide (Bhati and McDonnell 2020). Other social media fundraising campaigns have also been immensely successful (Lacetera, Macis, and Mele 2016; Slovic et al. 2017).

Saxton and Wang (2014) argue that social media is ideal for fundraising and philanthropy. First, it is suitable for targeting small donors through crowdfunding. Second, it enables peer-to-peer fundraising through solicitation to potential donors from people they trust in their social networks such as friends and family members. Third, social media makes it convenient for donors to use peer pressure to encourage others in their network to donate. For instance, Lacetera, Macis, and Mele (2016) found a positive relationship between broadcasting an individual's donation on Facebook and other gifts to a nonprofit.

Social media also enables us to better hear marginalized voices in the field of philanthropy. Scholars are now seeking to ascertain how people understand generosity in non-Western settings (Fowler and Mati 2019; Wiepking 2021). Social media provides scholars with a unique opportunity to perceive these marginalized groups' voices. For example, Zhou and Le Han (2019) used Internet discussions to discover the understudied grassroots philanthropy in China.

It is essential to allow more room for these voices. Research suggests that giving voice to subordinate groups can help change the dominant discourse (Chamberlain 1990; Varghese 2015). Scholars stress that we need more voices to apprise us of how philanthropy can create solutions to social problems and serve the public good (Eikenberry and Kluver 2004). Social media is a new channel for subordinate groups to speak out and be heard and can pave new pathways to "give voice to the voiceless." Moreover, on social media, subordinate groups can challenge the authority of traditionally dominant discourses (Zhou and Le Han 2019).

Social Media and Religion

Like the printing press did in the past, social media is significantly influencing society's beliefs and culture. It gives many people a lens through which they can view the world and its actions and is increasingly influencing people's beliefs about consumerism, politics, community, and religion, with the latter becoming embedded in people's religious traditions worldwide. Social media activities, thus, have become part of our religious understanding. Religious actors, whether organizations or prominent religious leaders who have an active presence on social media, including Pope Francis and the Dalai Lama, see social media as a critical tool for promoting religious actions.

Social media is affecting religion in two significant ways. First, it is helping to expand and create religious communities, and an increasing number of religious adherents and scholars are turning to social media to create forums to connect with their followers (Verschoor-Kirss 2012). For example, social media has taken over many of institutionalized religions' cultural and social functions and provides spiritual guidance, moral orientation, and a sense of belonging (Hjarvard 2011). Also, more and more religious scholars are turning to social media to motivate individuals toward religious acts such as visiting a church, praying regularly, and keeping an eye on the wellbeing of people of faith (Bobkowski and Pearce 2011; Everton 2019). These forums include sermons of clerics on YouTube and other platforms like Twitter to encourage people to act religiously (Kgatle 2018).

People are also increasingly using social media for proselytization. In a recent survey in the United Kingdom, 83 percent of Christians agreed the Internet is a place for proselytization, and 65 percent said they intentionally share their faith online in an attempt to encourage others to act religiously (Brubaker and Haigh 2017). Therefore, social media has become an important, if not the primary, source for the dissemination of religious issues, with spiritual knowledge and experiences being molded according to the demands of certain media genres, particularly tweets, Instagram posts, and Snapchats.

Second, social media is becoming a key platform for the diffusion of religious ideas and practices. While traditionally religious leaders have monopolized religious discussions on traditional media like television and radio, today social media is becoming a platform for everyday people to discuss spiritual issues and their opinions about religion. Therefore, increasingly people are turning to social media to discuss major religious issues that affect their lives, as well as for children's religious instruction materials that parents view as alternatives to religious schools. Additionally, "media muftis" dispense spiritual advice on radio and television call-in or write-in shows (J. W. Anderson 2003).

Social Media and Religious Giving

Initially, researchers were skeptical about religious organizations' adoption of social media, especially because religious organizations historically have been slow to adopt new technologies. Recent studies, however, have put those doubts to rest. Religious leaders have been some of the most innovative social media adopters. For instance, some churches use microblogging to circulate "faith memes." In other cases, churches have even created special "Twitter Sundays" to prompt members to tweet their reflections and questions throughout the service (Cheong 2012). Some religious leaders have been even more successful than celebrities in generating social media responses. For instance, one prominent priest, Fr. Meyer, was receiving more responses from his followers than Justin Bieber was (O'Leary 2012). Plainly, ample evidence suggests highly successful adoption of social media among religious organizations (H. A. Campbell 2012).

Social Media and Zakat

Several examples in the literature illustrate how individuals are using social media to interpret Islamic practices. For instance, in Indonesia, social media groups like the Great Muslimah are helping young Indonesians form their opinions about the characteristics of a pious Muslim. Similarly, a group called Pejuang Subuh (Morning Fighters) is using several social media platforms like WhatsApp to influence the group members' understanding of the importance of morning prayer in their lives (Slama 2018).

Relevant to zakat, the literature suggests that Muslims are using social media to discuss zakat in several ways. First, several organizations are using these channels for fundraising. It is noteworthy that while today annual zakat estimates are around $250 billion to $1 trillion (Alterman et al. 2005) Muslims often do not have sufficient information about the options for how to give zakat. For instance, several surveys across the Muslim world, including in Pakistan, Indonesia, Egypt, and Turkey, suggest that people often do not know of the opportunities to distribute their zakat (Adachi 2018) and give their zakat to the people closest to them. Thus, lack of information on zakat is a substantial issue for zakat fundraising. One of the main problems is use of the traditional method, which significantly limits public access to information, especially for corporate and government zakat institutions (Kasri and Putri 2018).

As a result, charities and government institutions that are increasingly responsible for collecting zakat have come to realize that social media is a great medium to inform people about the importance of zakat (Ridlwan and Sukmana 2018), to educate people about the amount of money they need to give, and to increase zakat literacy in general. Thus, more and more government zakat institutions and nonprofits are accelerating their outreach concerning zakat (Ammani, Abba, and Dandago 2014).

Second, while providing information about zakat practices, social media is also influencing how individuals understand the zakat method of giving. For instance, some charities are using social media to reinterpret how Islamic charity is perceived and practiced in Indonesia today, breaking with future promises of salvation and development and instead emphasizing the immediate benefits of giving (Kailani and Slama 2020). Islamic charities are also using social media to document their activities and attract funding. In doing so, they often project an image of real-time response to people in need and quick allocation of the funds they receive (Kailani and Slama 2020).

In addition to allowing charities to reinterpret the meaning of zakat, social media is also enabling citizens to discuss best practices for collecting zakat. As an illustration, in Ghana, where the government has instituted a centralized system for zakat, citizens are using social media to discuss the merits of having a centralized zakat system (Weiss 2020). Some of these discussions on zakat are open to the effectiveness of zakat distribution. Instead, they often focus on the fundamental theological issue of who has the mandate to collect and distribute it (Weiss 2020). Overall, this finding fits the paradigm of social media democratizing the discussion of zakat, where non-scholars also use it to discuss their opinions of the system.

Zakat: Traditional Versus Instrumental

While zakat is one of the five pillars of Islam, several debates about its meaning and practices are ongoing even today. Weiss (2020) categorizes these debates in two broad camps: traditionalist and instrumentalist. The more traditionalist discourse focuses on Muslims' moral obligation toward paying zakat. Religious scholars often articulate this perspective during their sermons, reminding Muslims of their obligation to pay zakat as part of their religion. This perspective does not focus on how the zakat is distributed or on the impact zakat can have on removing poverty in the world. From this perspective, the collection and distribution of zakat is primarily a personal affair, and this perspective focuses primarily on an individual's obligation to pay zakat rather than the impact its collection can have on society.

This perspective of zakat is often the predominant idea about charity in the Muslim world (Roy 1994; Weiss 2020). It primarily focuses on the local giving of zakat. As a result, in surveys around the world Muslims often perceive zakat as a personal responsibility and therefore like to give locally. This school of thought argues that paying zakat and deciding its mode of distribution is contingent on the individual, who chooses not only if and how he or she pays zakat, but also its amount and the causes for donation. To a certain extent, this idea relates to the notion that the religious act reflects an individual rather than a collective act. It also focuses primarily on theological and religious reasons for giving zakat rather than focusing on its socioeconomic potential.

The second discourse focuses on the semiprivate-public communal way of collecting and distributing zakat. This perspective finds poverty as the leading cause of the marginalization of Muslims. In contrast to the traditional discourse on zakat, which highlights the moral obligation to alleviate the sufferings of the poor and needy, the instrumentalist discourse highlights the social need of zakat as an instrument for poverty alleviation. It argues that zakat, if appropriately used, can reduce poverty in the Muslim world. Therefore, this perspective finds zakat as "the Muslim solution for eradicating misery and poverty" and a tool to ease Muslim communities' social and economic development. As a result, it is critical of the haphazard and local giving of zakat. Instead, it claims that local giving is random and is not achieving reduction of poverty.

This perspective offers several ways to look at zakat as an essential way of reducing poverty in the Muslim world. For instance, one way of looking at zakat is by conceptualizing it as social capital, which encourages cooperation, lowers transaction costs, and promotes a sense of responsibility toward others (Tlemsani and Matthews 2013). This perspective links it to social justice, with connections to the ideology of liberation theology. In this perspective, zakat can be the way to remove poverty in the Muslim world (Timani and Ashton 2019).

It focuses on the best-institutionalized way to remove zakat, either through the government or other nongovernmental institutions. This lens analyzes zakat as a social mechanism. Some economists in the Muslim world are also increasingly embracing the idea of using zakat as a mechanism for social growth and removing social inequity (Adachi 2018; Kuran 1997; Tlemsani and Matthews 2013).

STUDYING ZAKAT THROUGH TWITTER

Twitter provides unique data because of the sheer size of its data. Because of this issue, nonprofit scholars often restrict their analyses to smaller subsamples of the data. To address this issue, we employ machine learning (ML) methods in this study. Machine learning methods employ computer algorithms to categorize a text by looking at frequently co-occurring words (Wilkerson and Casas 2017; Anastasopoulos and Whitford 2019). Several recent papers have leveraged machine learning to understand patterns from large datasets for nonprofit studies (Ma, Jing, and Han 2018; Lecy and Thornton 2015; Litofcenko, Karner, and Maier 2020; Fyall, Moore, and Gugerty 2018; Ma and Konrath 2018; Suárez, Husted, and Casas 2018; Santos, Laureano, and Moro 2019).

In this study, we employ unsupervised machine learning methods. These methods attempt to discover the main topics or themes in a text by looking at co-occurring word clusters (Quinn et al. 2010; Grimmer and King 2011). After the model finds a set of co-occurring words, researchers interpret and label these topics. For example, a researcher can construe a collection of terms such as "Latinos," "Muslims," and "border" as an immigration topic. In addition to looking at the frequently occurring words, researchers interpret these topics by looking at each topic's examples.

We employed the structural topical model (STM), a probabilistic topic model. STM is a mixed-membership model, meaning that it considers each document to be a mixture of various topics. Scholars use STM in several domains, including studying corporate branding (Serôdio, McKee, and Stuckler 2018), human rights texts (Bagozzi and Berliner 2018), as well as political blogs (Chuang et al. 2014). The main advantage of STM over other unsupervised models is that it can incorporate document-level external covariates into the prior distributions for document topics or topic words. It effectively allowed us to estimate regression models that treated each identified topic's prevalence as an "outcome variable" of the explanatory variables. Scholars have recently discovered STM's utility for nonprofit research. For instance, Wasif (2021) employed it to study newspapers' framing of Muslim nonprofits. Other research outside nonprofit studies have used it to explore Twitter datasets (Garcia-Rudolph et al. 2019; Aslett et al. 2020; Mishler et al. 2015).

Data Collection

Our rationale was to search for tweets that mentioned zakat, but restrict the search to those in the English language, which led to the collection of 100,000 tweets. After identifying a tweet, we found that many were very repetitive. To eliminate these tweets, we removed all the duplicates.

After going through the primary process, we cleaned up the texts using traditional pre-processing methods, such as removing retweets, hashtags, etc. We also performed several other germane steps, including stemming the tweets. Then we used the STM R package to find the best-suited topics for the tweets. Based on criteria employed by other scholars, we chose articles based on exclusivity and semantic coherence (Wasif 2021). We ended up with 20 topics. To understand each topic, we looked at the FREX and most frequently occurring words. In addition, to better understand the issues, we looked at examples of each topic. After discovering each topic, we further categorized the topics under the instrumentalist or traditionalist framework.

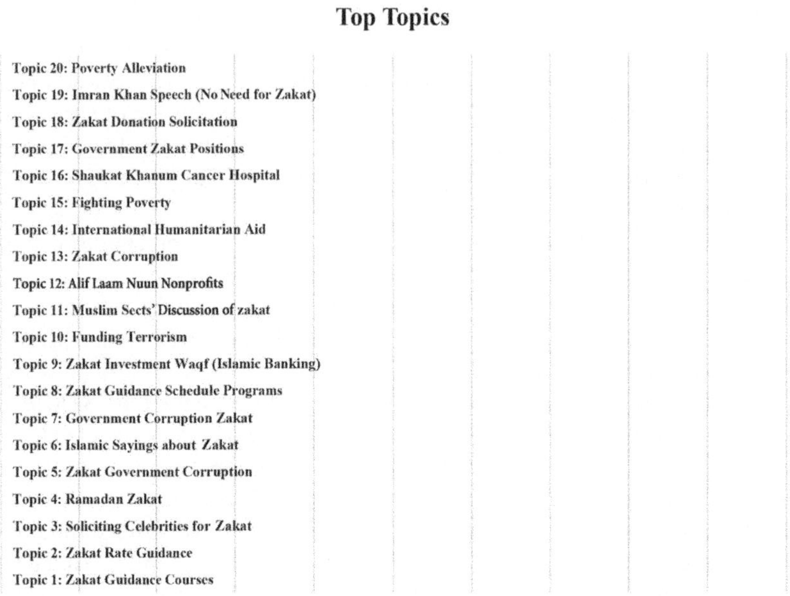

Top Topics

Topic 20: Poverty Alleviation

Topic 19: Imran Khan Speech (No Need for Zakat)

Topic 18: Zakat Donation Solicitation

Topic 17: Government Zakat Positions

Topic 16: Shaukat Khanum Cancer Hospital

Topic 15: Fighting Poverty

Topic 14: International Humanitarian Aid

Topic 13: Zakat Corruption

Topic 12: Alif Laam Nuun Nonprofits

Topic 11: Muslim Sects' Discussion of zakat

Topic 10: Funding Terrorism

Topic 9: Zakat Investment Waqf (Islamic Banking)

Topic 8: Zakat Guidance Schedule Programs

Topic 7: Government Corruption Zakat

Topic 6: Islamic Sayings about Zakat

Topic 5: Zakat Government Corruption

Topic 4: Ramadan Zakat

Topic 3: Soliciting Celebrities for Zakat

Topic 2: Zakat Rate Guidance

Topic 1: Zakat Guidance Courses

Figure 4.1   Top topics

Traditional discourse

Several topics fell under the traditional zakat discourse, as shown here:

- Topic 1: Zakat Guidance Courses
- Topic 2: Zakat Rate Guidance
- Topic 4: Ramadan Zakat
- Topic 6: Islamic Sayings about Zakat
- Topic 8: Zakat Guidance Schedule Programs
- Topic 11: Muslim Sects' Discussion of Zakat

These topics focused on the moral obligation of individual zakat giving. Some cases asked for the clergy's expertise about zakat giving or discussed zakat's importance in Islam. Other topics focused on the religious duty to provide zakat by citing specific holy verses. One topic (Muslim Sects' Discussion of Zakat) showed that ordinary individuals talk about zakat in their daily lives, but that was the only topic they ordinarily discussed.

Both Topic 1 (Zakat Guidance Courses) and Topic 2 (Zakat Rate Guidance) provided broad scholarly guidance on zakat matters. Likewise, Topic 8 (Zakat Guidance Schedule Programs) provided the time and date for a scholar's programs on zakat. Together these three topics offered guidance on the amount and methods of giving zakat.

The following tweet is an excellent example of a Zakat Guidance Course (Topic 1): "Zakat made simple a practical guide this course aims to teach today's Muslim the practical essentials of paying zakat in an informed, responsible manner. #Ramadan #Zakat #Kiflayn #practicalguide #responsible #payyourzakat."

Similarly, under Topic 2 (Zakat Rate Guidance), scholars shed light on the eligibility criteria (nisab) for giving zakat. For example: "Zakat Nisab Gold date 15th Rabi-ul-Awwal 1440h 23rd November 2018 Zakat Nisab n1,117 200 dowry theft n13 965 blood money diyyah 55, 860 000 Source: Islamictimingandresearch.org." In addition, Topic 8 (Zakat Guidance Schedule Programs) often provided the time and venue for a scholar's zakat program. The following tweet is a good example:

> Saturday 7th Dec at 4 pm
>   Bulugh-ul-Maram
>   Book of Zakat
>   Chapter of Sadaqah
>   Division of sadaqah
>   Lesson 17
>   Broadcast live.

Other tweets focused on the religious importance of zakat. For instance, Topic 6 (Islamic Sayings about Zakat) provided Islamic quotes from religious texts about zakat. The following tweet discussed the importance of zakat as one of the fundamental pillars of Islam:

> Islam is based on five pillars
>   To testify that none has the right to be worshipped but Allah Muhammad is Allah's Apostle (PBUH)
>   To offer the compulsory prayers
>   To observe fast during the month of Ramadan
>   To pay zakat
>   To perform pilgrimage to Mecca.

We found that most tweets focused on the scholarly interpretation of zakat's importance in Muslims' lives. However, Topic 11 (Muslim Sects' Discussion of Zakat) provided some evidence that non-scholars discuss how different sects may reinterpret zakat. For example, the following tweet discusses Pakistani banks' deduction of zakat for Ahmadis and Shias: "If you give an affidavit in a Pakistani bank that you are Shia, they don't deduct zakat. I am merely mentioning the legal status nothing against Shia or Ahmedi."

Instrumentalist definition of zakat

According to Weiss (2020), the instrumentalist role of zakat focuses on the position it can play in eliminating societal problems. It focuses on the socio-economic position of zakat in poverty alleviation. Several topics, given below, fell under this category:

- Topic 3: Soliciting Celebrities for Zakat
- Topic 4: Ramadan Zakat
- Topic 5: Zakat Government Corruption
- Topic 7: Government Corruption Zakat
- Topic 9: Zakat Investment Waqf (Islamic Banking)
- Topic 10: Funding Terrorism
- Topic 12: Alif Laam Nuun Noprofits (Specific Nonprofit)
- Topic 13: Zakat Corruption
- Topic 14: International Humanitarian Aid
- Topic 15: Fighting Poverty
- Topic 16: Shaukat Khanum Cancer Hospital (a hospital for free cancer care in Pakistan that receives zakat)
- Topic 17: Government Zakat Positions
- Topic 18: Zakat Donation Solicitation
- Topic 19: Imran Khan Speech (No Need for Zakat)
- Topic 20: Poverty Alleviation

Charities and individuals were using social media to solicit donations. For instance, under Topic 3 (Soliciting Celebrities for Zakat), a user tweeted to solicit celebrities such as ex-Pakistani Cricketer Saqlain Mushtaq for zakat. Here is an excellent example of this type of tweet:

> Assalamualekum (Islamic Greeting) Saqlain Mushtaq brother I am Dehli in India Plz [sic: Please] help my family Plz I trust you I am no fraud [sic: fraud] no fee [sic: fake] plz help me zakat Khairaat Sadka
>   help my family my email id contact [sic: contact] you my family problem
>   Send you plz
>   (email id of the person)
>   Plz I traust [sic: trust] you plz plz plz help.

Additionally, charities were using Twitter heavily to solicit zakat for their work. As an illustration, Topic 4 (Ramadan Zakat) focused on raising the largest amount of zakat during the holy month of Ramadan. An excellent example of a zakat Ramadan tweet is the following:

> Last ten days of Ramadan
>   Maximize your reward by saving lives
>   with your zakat and donations, Pakistan children's health foundation can save thousands of children born with health diseases #chd #savelives #donate #zakat #ramzan2018 #pchf #chdawareness.

Interestingly, one topic focused on new online methods for giving zakat. The following tweet expresses information about using an app for giving zakat. This tweet provides information about an app to channel zakat to a Mufti (religious scholar):

> Zakat smart app provides a VIP service where you can request a Mufti to answer your inquiries about your zakat and zakat companies
>   Download the zakatsmart app from the Apple store and play store
>   #zakatpayment #zakatfund #zakatvipservice #vipservice.

Zakat target areas

Several topics focused on the uses of zakat. For instance, Topic 14 included zakat's role in helping with humanitarian aid. The following two tweets show the work of one organization (Zakat Foundation) helping with humanitarian aid in both the United States and abroad (Palestine): "Chicago Jan 30 Zakat Foundation of America staff braved the coldest arctic weather in a century to hand out thousands of blankets, coats, hats, socks, warm meals, water and hygiene kits to Chicago's homeless"; "In Gaza Zakat Foundation worked to support specialized programs for youth affected with Post-traumatic stress disorder Ptsd."

Topic 15 focused on asking for zakat for poverty elimination. The following tweet exemplifies this topic:

> Prince Educational Appeal for Zakat the implementation of humanitarian and development programs to fight poverty around the kindly come ahead for prince educational society a/c number *****
>   Canara Bank Mozzamjahi Market Branch Hyderabad Telangana Ifsc ****.

Similarly, Topic 20 (Poverty Alleviation) examined the role of zakat in removing poverty:

> #Helpinghandsforpoor
>   Zakat and charity is the best way to help the poor.
>   Just 2.5 of your savings can change the lives of the poor and the needy
>   Pay your zakat to Zakat India
>   To support checkout.

Furthermore, another topic (Shaukat Khanum Cancer Hospital) dealt with zakat's role in supplying free cancer treatment. These tweets focused on the Shaukat Khanum Cancer Hospital, the largest free cancer treatment hospital in Pakistan (which was set up by Imran Khan, a former prime minister of Pakistan, before he became the prime minister):

> Skmch [sic: Shaukat Khanum Cancer Hospital] RC fund meter
> Last 5 days left to complete this year's target
> So far, we have achieved 96 of our budget the budget of skmch (Shaukat Khanum Cancer Hospital) for the year 2018 is Rs 11 billion half of it is raised through your donations and zakat
> Donate generously.

One of the topics, Zakat Investment Waqf (Islamic Banking), involved the possibility of using zakat for investment opportunities. This topic focused on several new people in Islamic economics, suggesting that it is possible to use zakat and Islamic charity to achieve social and economic growth if done strategically. Thus, instead of thinking of zakat as merely charity to help the poor, one group of tweets considered the possibility of viewing it as an investment fund:

> Funding is critical to further SDG achievement stakeholders in Malaysia must look at innovative solutions such as Islamic finance instruments such as Zakat Waqf Sukuk HSBC Amanah's world's 1st SDG Sukuk shows Islamic finance has a huge role to play in the financing of SDGs.

Government and zakat
In most of the Muslim world, the government plays a role in collecting zakat. Therefore, unsurprisingly, several tweets discussed the role of government in zakat collection. For instance, Topic 17 (Government Zakat Positions) focused on supplying updates about the activities of government zakat officials. The following tweet provided information about the chairman of the Zakat Central Board (a government position in Pakistan) who attended a wedding ceremony:

> President District Central PPP Karachi Adv Zafar Ahmed Siddiqi and Chairman Zakat District Central Karachi Mr. Abdul Samad Gabol attended a wedding ceremony of cousins of Sardar Samad Baloch Shehzad Majeed Baloch Information Secretary District Central PPP Karachi.

Topic 19 (Imran Khan Speech) focused on addresses by former Pakistani Prime Minister Imran Khan. He said that he envisioned that no one in Pakistan will need charity or zakat money anymore. The country would be rich enough to pay zakat to other countries:

> My vision is that day when we will not have people who will need Zakat we will inshallah be country that will help other countries in need maybe I won't even be alive till that time, but that is my vision that is Pakistan. I want to see Pakistan zindabad
> #pmikaddress.

Corruption practices

Several tweets expressed frustration about corruption with zakat funds. For instance, one topic included a discussion about Imran Khan embezzling zakat. The following tweet about government corruption suggested that Imran Khan Niazi, a former Pakistani prime minister, eats zakat illegally, is a thief, and is stealing zakat for his benefit: "Shameful Niazi chore (thief) zakat khore (eater)." Another tweet also implied that Imran Khan stole zakat money: "One and only pioneer of offshore companies ... zakat chour (thief) Money Launderer ... the product of dictator Pervaiz Musharraf."

Similarly, Topic 13 (Zakat Corruption) included tweets blaming Imran Khan for eating zakat money for personal gain. The tweet, written in mixed Urdu, noted that Imran Khan had bought a house and other expensive items for personal aggrandizement out of money targeted for zakat:

> Naturally its [sic: it's] a joke for you because U [sic: you] are sitting in a free house bought by haram paisa tum log ghareeb ko 2000 mey votes key liye khareed leteho tum sey diff Khuda k log hein jo 5 marla Ghar Bana ker dene per tayar hey khaney ki adat Sirf noonies ko hey jo Sara zakat kaohgai?
> (Translation of preceding tweet: Naturally, it is a joke for you because you are sitting in a house bought by illegal money. You buy poor people's vote for Rs 2000. There are people of God who are different from you who live on five Marla's house (tiny houses). It is not only Muslim League (N) (the opposition party) who is corrupt. How much zakat money will you embezzle?)

Interestingly, only Topic 10 (Funding Terrorism) connected zakat to any kind of terrorism. For instance, the tweet below suggested that buying halal meat meant people fund terrorist groups and associated it with the Muslim Brotherhood:

> All UK supermarkets are registered with the Halal food authority. This means that all products have the halal tax levied on them the customer pays 2.5 zakat tax which is used for jihad, and your potential death boycott all supermarkets, 2.5 of turnover goes to Muslim Brotherhood.

DISCUSSION

Our analysis indicates that social media discusses zakat in instrumentalist and traditional frameworks. While focusing on the religious importance of zakat and informing traditional sources and scholars about the necessity of zakat, it also emphasizes the use of zakat for improving several societal problems. The results show that tweets discuss the potential of zakat for reducing poverty and supplying humanitarian aid and services across the globe. Additionally, social media highlights zakat's potential to help resolve health issues in the Muslim world, especially concerning the Shaukat Khanum Cancer Hospital in Pakistan founded by Imran Khan. Notably, an entire topic focused on the potential for zakat not only as a charity but also as a financial investment.

Together, the results of the topics in this study indicate that users want to use zakat for several purposes. Some tweets also discuss the role of zakat in governmental affairs. However, they often focus on the use of zakat for corruption practices. Primarily, they focus on Imran Khan, who, before becoming prime minister, ran a zakat-funded cancer hospital. Many tweets implied that he may have used the hospital for corrupt practices.

The findings show little evidence that Twitter is used for theological debates and reinterpreting the theological understanding of zakat by non-scholars, that is, ordinary people, with minimal religious discussions on the meaning of zakat. However, Twitter users often employ it to discuss the best priorities for using zakat. Thus, it seems likely that Twitter users want to discuss zakat's meaning in modern-day society and not focus on its religious meaning and interpretation.

The study also shows that charities use social media to ask for zakat for their work. Additionally, the study provides information about channeling zakat to the Muslim world through apps and other electronic means. Interestingly, some individual users are using Twitter to ask for charity. This finding is like the use of other forums, such as GoFundMe, that individuals use to help their causes. Despite Islamophobic discourse that often tries to portray zakat and Islamic charity negatively, only one topic associates zakat with terrorism of any sort.

Overall, rather than minimizing the role of traditional sources and authorities, social media is helping them increase their role on religious matters. There is little evidence to suggest that social media helps non-scholars appear as authentic sources for reinterpreting their role in zakat. Thus, only some primary theological debates occur about zakat and its reinterpretation.

On the other hand, social media is providing charities with an effective forum for requesting zakat. These charities request zakat for several reasons, including poverty elimination, health care, and humanitarian aid. There is some discussion about the role of zakat in investment. However, most tweets focused on its traditional role as a poverty eliminator rather than as a new investment method. Social media also provides a forum for people to discuss concerns about the misuse and embezzlement of zakat. This finding is notable as it agrees with other literature that has examined the critical issue of abuse in charitable giving.

CONCLUSION

Overall, we find a highly active Twitter sphere on zakat. There are several similarities and dissimilarities in these discussions and Western ideas of charity. In Western countries, the government generally does not collect charity. However, in the case of zakat, social media discusses the role of government in zakat collection. Moreover, in the Western context, we do not often consider zakat mandatory. However, in the case of Muslims, tweets refer to nisab (a compulsory giving).

In other ways, Twitter's discourse on zakat is fundamentally different from the mainstream discourse of philanthropy. For instance, the discussion on zakat not only focuses on how it will benefit the receiver but also strongly focuses on how the zakat giver also benefits from giving zakat; while the mainstream view on charitable giving often focuses on organizational or institutional factors, such as efficiency, effectiveness, management, and governance. On the other hand, zakat discourse focuses more on how it benefits the individual, emphasizing individual motivation and personal gain. While the mainstream discourse advocates for practices that will increase the efficiency and effectiveness of the charitable sector, zakat discourse focuses more on how it will improve an individual's religious standing.

Moreover, while mainstream discourse focuses on the funding advocacy purposes of nonprofits, advocacy does not appear as a vital concern for individuals. Similarly, there has been little focus on the use of zakat to advance civil rights or democracy. It seems that in Western countries, charity and charitable giving also relate to power and resources; motivations for zakat include either fulfilling one's religious self or using zakat for service-providing purposes, such as health care and poverty.

On the other hand, there are several similarities between zakat's discussion and mainstream discourse. For one, like charity, social media users consider zakat as a critical element in poverty elimination. They also discuss the potential use of zakat for several purposes, including poverty relief and health care. Some tweets about zakat discuss its role in financing, such as ideas about social entrepreneurship and using zakat for investment purposes.

At the same time, the very nature of technology is changing the collection of zakat. Like mainstream organizations, charities and individuals are using new electronic channels to collect zakat. Social media tools are also helping charities and scholars create awareness and knowledge about zakat giving. Thus, Twitter can be a convenient tool for organizations trying to increase their traditional zakat base and reach new audiences. It may also be a convenient tool for Islamic financing institutions like Islamic banks to persuade people to invest zakat funds for social entrepreneurship purposes and to help people build sustainable livelihoods rather than giving them only charity. Social media tools may also offer a valuable forum for individuals looking for help as well as people who may help.

Social media also provides a forum to discuss issues of zakat corruption. Thus, they can highlight the corruption issues in government or other entities that are collecting these funds. Therefore, it may also serve as an extra check on these institutions and highlight the main corruption issues.

Limitations

The data used in this study have several limitations, as they focus primarily on tweets from 2018 through 2019, which means we were unable to discuss zakat in the context of COVID-19. Similarly, we focused on Twitter; therefore, we do not know how other forums are talking about zakat. By focusing on the English language, we did not account for discussions in other languages. Future studies could conduct comparative analyses to address how different platforms, such as WhatsApp and other media, discuss zakat in this context, which would enhance the existing knowledge on this topic. It may be important also to see the discussions of zakat in a non-English language.

5. The practice of sadaqa in Muslim America

> And spend [in the way of Allah] from what We have provided you before death approaches one of you and he says, "My Lord, if only You would delay me for a brief term so I would give charity and be among the righteous."
>
> Qur'an 63:10

Sadaqa comprises different practices of Muslim giving, including zakat, as well as a broad range of practices that include giving non-zakat money, volunteering, and informal acts of philanthropy such as smiling, advocating for the oppressed, among others. Therefore, sadaqa includes formal and informal giving and acts of generosity and encompasses a wide range of Muslim practices.

In this chapter, we focus on the Muslim-American practices of sadaqa drawing from historical examples and new data from the 2022 Muslim-American Giving survey. With a particular focus on current Muslim philanthropic practices regarding sadaqa, we examine the broad philanthropic patterns of Muslim-American giving. We do so, first, by defining sadaqa and looking at the overall monetary giving for both faith-based causes and non-faith-based causes among Muslims. We then examine the volunteering practices among Muslim-American populations and compare those practices with those of the general population. Next, we test whether Muslims are willing to embrace a broader conception of philanthropy in their sadaqa practices than the general population. Overall, we find a broad embrace of the sadaqa among Muslim Americans. Not only do they give generously and volunteer more than the general population, but they are also significantly more likely to embrace a broader set of actions as part of their philanthropic practices than the general population. We then present case studies of sadaqa practices, then examine the data related to Muslim-American giving to help illustrate how broadly Muslims practice sadaqa.

DEFINING SADAQA

Sadaqa is the most general and capacious term used in Muslim philanthropy. In ordinary usage, sadaqa refers to voluntary, extemporaneous acts of "beneficent giving," distinguishing it from the obligatory practice of zakat or alms (Singer

2018, 18). Zakat is listed as one of the five pillars of Islamic worship alongside praying, fasting during Ramadan, going on pilgrimages, and attesting to the oneness of God and Muhammad as God's messenger. Sadaqa has historically and continues to play an important role in Muslim societies and communities' textual traditions and practices.

The word sadaqa asserts an extensive definition of philanthropy The tri-lateral verbal root that composes the word sadaqa (s-d-q or ص د ق) occurs 155 times in the Qur'an across 19 derived verbal and noun forms and appears as a reference to charity 24 times (*Quran Dictionary* 2017). While this root can mean "charity" or "to give charity," it can also mean "to be truthful," "to accept or believe the truth," and "to attest." In this sense, sadaqa connotes more than just the voluntary giving of money to various charitable causes but extends into the ethical realm of virtuous action, going beyond donations to include doing good in one's speech and actions, avoiding harm, rebuking what is considered evil, and even smiling.

Recorded narrations of the Prophet Mohammad attest to this wide understanding of publicly beneficial action. According to one hadith, "The Prophet (ﷺ) said, 'Enjoining, all that is good is a sadaqa'" (Bukhari n.d.) Elsewhere, the Qur'an emphasizes that all who work toward the good find God's favor: "But pardon them and overlook [their misdeeds]. Indeed, Allāh loves the doers of good" (Qur'an 5:13). Thus, forgiveness is an act of charity that all can participate in, regardless of their means.

While Muslims today often distinguish between obligatory alms (zakat) and extemporaneous, voluntary acts of charity (sadaqa), this distinction becomes much fuzzier when we look closely at the terminology in the Qur'an, which at times uses sadaqa to refer to what Muslim interpretive traditions have understood to mean zakat. In Qur'an 9:60, God specifies eight eligible categories to which one should give their zakat including to the poor, the needy, orphans, travelers, and more. Importantly, the word used in this verse is sadaqa and not zakat. Elsewhere in the Qur'an (2:110), God commands the believer to pray and give obligatory charity as two equally significant acts of worship. In this verse, the word zakat is used directly. Here, we have two instances in which zakat is commanded but two different words are used to specify the same act. Thus, scholars have identified sadaqa to be a more general term that can at times refer to both obligatory giving of 2.5 percent of one's wealth (zakat) and acts of spontaneous or voluntary charity (sadaqa al- al-tatawwuʿ) (Weir and Zysow 2012).

The Arabic word sadaqa is a cognate of the Hebrew term *tzedakah*, and both derive from a shared semitic root. The Arabic, Hebrew, and Aramaic meanings of the term are similarly broad, connoting gifts and alms as well as notions of justice and righteousness (Singer 2008, 4). Frederick Bird (1982) noted that in Israelite religion and early Judaism, tzedakah signified an ethical practice and a set of normative social relations. Tzedakah, like sadaqa, is not simply "charity," but a communal worship commanded by God to construct responsible and just socioeconomic relationships in an unequal world. Bird said, "[Tzedakah], which referred to attributes of God as well as to human virtues, meant 'righteousness' and 'graciousness.' God required [tzedakah] of his people, namely rightly ordered human relations that did not neglect those who were disadvantaged" (148).

Sadaqa can be formal (giving to institutions) or informal (giving to individuals). Sadaqa (like zakat) need not take place through third-sector organizations like NPOs or NGOs, and, in fact, across most of the world it is given informally to family members and neighbors or anonymously dropped into boxes at shrines and mosques to feed the poor. There are no limitations on sadaqa, either maximums or minimums, and it is presumed that most non-zakat charity by Muslims falls within this category. This includes both required and voluntary forms of philanthropy.

There are many prophetic narrations concerning the importance of charity toward all of creation. In one narration, a companion of the Prophet, Abu Hurairah, reported:

> [The] Messenger of Allah (ﷺ) said, "While a man was walking on his way, he became extremely thirsty. He found a well, he went down into it to drink water. Upon leaving it, he saw a dog which was panting out of thirst. His tongue was lolling out and he was eating moist earth from extreme thirst. The man thought to himself: 'This dog is extremely thirsty as I was.' So he descended into the well, filled up his leather sock with water, and holding it in his teeth, climbed up and quenched the thirst of the dog. Allah appreciated his action and forgave his sins." The companions asked: "Shall we be rewarded for showing kindness to the animals also?" He (ﷺ) said, "A reward is given in connection with every living creature." (Imam al-Nawawi n.d.)

In some hadith that we have already discussed in another chapter, we find that sadaqa can take many forms. Those who can afford it can give off their wealth, and those with nothing can give sadaqa by helping others, doing good, and abstaining from evil. Thus, all Muslims, regardless of their financial status or physical ability, can participate in the spiritual rewards accompanied with performing acts of charity.

Sadaqa as Informal Philanthropy

Sadaqa as a concept provides a broad, holistic understanding of giving, including monetary giving and embracing a range of informal and formal practices. Academic scholarship and philanthropic best practices increasingly emphasize the need to define philanthropy beyond numbers (for more on this topic, see the section "Philanthropy Beyond Numbers" later in the chapter). Particularly, a growing number of scholars define and categorize philanthropy as acts beyond the scope of formal institutions such as NGOs, NPOs, and foundations.

Recent scholars have attempted to provide a broader definition of philanthropy by emphasizing "informal philanthropy," which can comprise a broader set of practices, especially in Muslim philanthropic spaces. Osei and Alagidede (2022) defined informal philanthropy as donating money and goods to neighbors, friends, and extended family members, which could also include a broader range of acts such as volunteering for different causes as well as in-kind giving—that is, donating nonmonetary goods or services for a charitable purpose.

There is increasing recognition that with a more inclusive definition of philanthropy, we will continue to appreciate the philanthropic efforts across cultures. Furthermore, by not systematically including informal philanthropy, we will continue to underestimate the philanthropic contributions of the poorest and most marginalized communities globally. Charitable practices are not the exclusive domain of the upper and middle classes, but also belong to the poorest among us.

The scope of informal philanthropy

Informal philanthropy is more widespread than the formal philanthropic practice of giving large monetary gifts, and it may even constitute the social fabric and everyday lives of those without means (Heist et al. 2021; Siddiqui 2022; Wilkinson-Maposa et al. 2005). Moreover, scholars have noted that it has been and still is more prevalent in countries outside the Western world (Everett, Haque, and Rand 2016; Fowler and Mati 2019; Heist et al. 2021). If informality is the dominant mode of philanthropic behavior around the world, it poses significant challenges to the overemphasis on donors and major gifts as we are not focusing on a major section of global philanthropic practices (Brinkerhoff 2014; Fateh Ahmad and Majid 2021b; Heist et al. 2021; Einolf 2017).

Nevertheless, scholars now realize that informal giving is spreading across the globe and that, in fact, such practices are becoming more and more common worldwide (Einolf 2017). For instance, García-Colín and Ruz (2016) found that 51.2 percent of Mexicans gave money to people they knew personally. In South Africa, 45 percent reported giving informally (Everatt et al. 2005). Similarly, most of the philanthropy in India is conducted informally (Heist et al. 2021).

Researchers have used various tools to measure informal philanthropy. Heist et al. (2021) measured altruism by asking people questions about their monetary donations, their giving of food, and their volunteerism. Fateh Ahmad and Majid (2021b) focused on a household's reported monetary value of charitable donations to individuals (as opposed to organizations). García-Colín and

Ruz (2016) studied giving of in-kind contributions in order to assess the use of informal philanthropy, which they defined as nonmonetary giving. Taniguchi (2012) focused on volunteering for informal organizations (like family, extended family, and network of neighbors). Everatt et al. (2005) focused on giving money and time to the poor and extended family networks in order to assess informal philanthropy (Obadare and Krawczyk 2022).

Religious Volunteering

Volunteerism is a critical part of sadaqa. Most faith communities strongly value philanthropic acts of giving and volunteering. In fact, research suggests that religious people volunteer more than nonreligious people (Eckel and Grossman 2004, 272; Hustinx et al. 2014).

However, despite a long tradition of volunteering in Muslim societies, little literature has attempted to estimate its scope in the Muslim world. Unsurprisingly, most of the research on religious volunteerism has focused on Christian groups, with most suggesting that they volunteer extensively (Forbes and Zampelli 2014). However, demographics may impact the nature of volunteering; affiliation with specific denominations may predict motivation levels. Previous research indicates that Protestants volunteer more in America (Wuthnow 1991; Wilson 2000), possibly due to the nonhierarchical nature of Protestantism and its division into smaller parishes, which are more effective at social sanctioning (Dekker and Halman 2005).

There is limited research on volunteerism in the case of Muslims, but that research does suggest that Muslims do a significant amount of volunteering. Nearly one in ten Australians volunteer, and a 2016 survey showed that 9 percent of Australian Muslims volunteer, though this number may be higher, as it excluded informal volunteering (Peucker 2016).

Muslim-American Sadaqa Practices

Muslim Americans are often at the center of conversations in the US political and socioeconomic sphere. They are also one of the fastest growing groups in the United States, with approximately 1.1 percent of the US population belonging to the Muslim faith. A 2018 Pew survey projected that Muslim Americans will be the second largest faith-based group in the United States by 2040. Muslim Americans are also one of the most racially diverse groups in the United States, comprising Arabs, Asians, African Americans, and Caucasians. Latinos are currently one of the fastest growing Muslim-American groups as well (Mohamed 2018).

However, despite the increased growth of the Muslim population in the United States, scarce data-driven research exists on Muslim giving, and even less data and information are available on Muslim philanthropic practices, especially pertaining to sadaqa. Given the centrality of giving among Muslim communities and the vital role religious giving plays in philanthropy more broadly, it is worth taking a deeper look at how and why American Muslims give.

Thousands of nonprofit organizations nationwide support Muslim communities across a broad spectrum of needs. Although some funding for these needs flows from outside Muslim communities (from both individuals and foundations), such funds are limited, and most of the financing that supports the unique needs of Muslim communities still comes from Muslims themselves. Thus, a thorough investigation into the philanthropic practices of American Muslims is necessary as we consider the development and strengthening of the communities and the institutions that serve them. At the same time, it is also essential to understand the motivations behind Muslim giving, especially those that prompt them to give to specific causes.

AMERICAN MUSLIMS' PHILANTHROPIC MOTIVATIONS AND PRACTICES

To uncover the motivations and practices behind American Muslims' giving habits, the Lilly School of Philanthropy conducted a survey in collaboration with Islamic Relief USA that included a broad range of studies. The survey is unique because earlier surveys investigated only whether Muslims practiced philanthropy and gave to specific causes, making this survey the first one to attempt to identify Muslim charities' scope and to assess monetary support for various causes.

The study was a self-administered web survey conducted by Indiana University Lilly Family School of Philanthropy. The study investigated the opinions of Muslims and the general population regarding faith customs, donation practices and attitudes, volunteer work, COVID-19, uncertainty intolerance, financial wellbeing, and discrimination. The survey also looked at how Muslims made decisions about donations. SSRS conducted the survey from March 17 through April 7, 2021. The team surveyed 2,005 respondents, including 1,003 Muslim respondents and 1,002 general population respondents.

The survey found that Muslims give more to both faith- and non-faith-based causes than non-Muslims. If we extrapolate the overall giving to 3.45 million Muslims (based on Pew Survey), we find that Muslims gave approximately $4.3 billion. Muslims gave $1,810 to faith-based causes, compared with $1,138 in the general population. Again, if we extrapolate the average giving of Muslims to 3.45 million Muslims, we find that Muslims contributed $2.4 billion to faith-based giving. An average Muslim gave $1,400 to non-faith-based causes, compared with $767 in the general population. If we extrapolate it to 3.45 million, Muslims gave an estimated $1.9 billion for non-faith-based causes.[1] Moreover, we also find a broader range of Sadaqa practice among Muslims. For instance, we find that Muslims volunteer more than the general population. Additionally, we find that Muslims are also willing to embrace a broader definition of philanthropy in their philanthropic practices.

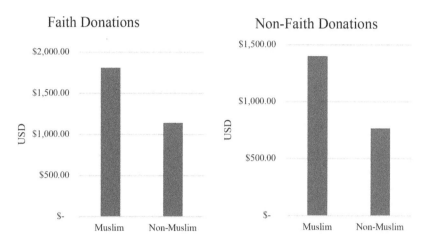

Figure 5.1   Comparison of monetary giving among Muslims and the general population

We also found that Muslims spend more hours volunteering every year than non-Muslims. Muslim Americans spend 66.61 hours volunteering for faith-based causes and 45.93 hours volunteering for non-faith-based causes, compared with 11.8 hours of faith-based volunteering and 13.72 hours for non-faith volunteering in the general population. These findings provide unique evidence that Muslims volunteer more than the general population.

Additionally, our findings suggest that American Muslims generously give their money and time in the United States, much more than the average population. In terms of preferences for giving to specific causes, Muslim-American preferences generally align with those of the general public. There are, however, some distinct differences. For instance, Muslims usually give a smaller proportion of their charity and volunteering to houses of worship or mosques (27.26 percent), compared with the average population (51.28 percent).

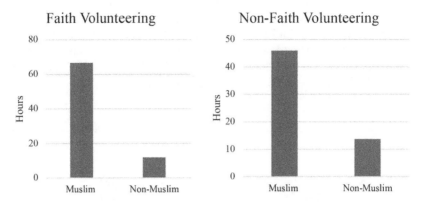

*Figure 5.2   Comparison of volunteering among Muslims and the general
            population*

American Muslim Spending within their Faith Community

When we looked at the preferences for giving among Muslims, we found that
Muslims' preferences for giving are generally similar to those of the general
population with some differences.

For example, giving to their houses of worship is a significant form of
giving for Muslims, as, on average, Muslims contribute 27.45 percent of their
faith-based charitable giving to houses of worship. Still, Muslims' giving to
houses of worship is lower than that of non-Muslims, who give 47.17 percent
of their faith-based charity to houses of worship.

Muslims also try to provide relief across the globe. In fact, Muslims report
providing a considerable proportion of their charitable giving to overseas relief
(12.81 percent), followed by domestic relief (11.13 percent), which is higher
than those by average Americans. In the Muslim community, it is commonly
thought that Muslims donate disproportionately to overseas relief, while
neglecting the needs of their immediate communities. However, we did not
find support for this belief. In fact, Muslims' giving to domestic relief is very
similar to that of the general population.

We did, however, find that Muslims spend more on civil rights protection
for the members of their community than any other faith group, with Muslims
directing nearly 8.47 percent of their contributions toward civil rights, compared with 5.31 percent of the general public. There is undoubtedly a need for
such protection, as Muslims continue to find themselves at the heart of national
security discussions and often face racism, xenophobia, and Islamophobia.
This situation may be based on the fact that a relatively high percentage of
American Muslims are immigrants, as half of all American Muslims were born

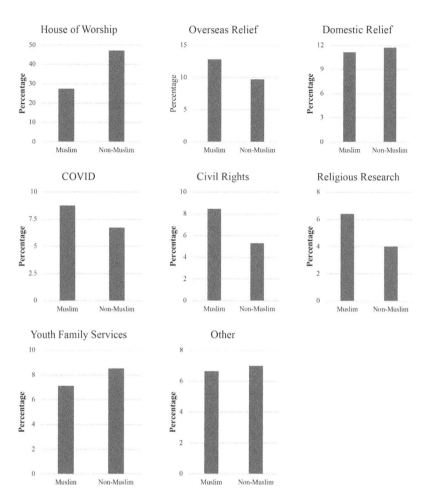

Figure 5.3   Preferences of giving among Muslims

in another country. Previous generations of newcomers to the United States faced similar threats to their civil liberties and went through periods when they had to fight to protect their communities. In that sense, although Muslims are outliers in this category at this moment in time, they may be falling in line with well-established (though unfortunate) historical precedents.

It is also interesting that Muslims, on average, direct 6.43 percent of their contributions to religious research, compared with 4.02 percent of the general population. This finding hints at a link between how marginalized a religious community can be and the need for more research and funding on that particular topic.

American Muslim Volunteering within their Faith Community

We found that, in general, the volunteering behavior of Muslims is similar
to their giving. Muslims spend less time volunteering for houses of worship
than the general population (23 percent versus 48 percent, respectively).
Interestingly, there were no large differences between Muslim volunteering
to either overseas or domestic relief and that of the general population. These
findings suggest that Muslims spend nearly an equal proportion of their time
on opportunities to volunteer for international and domestic relief.

Giving Preferences: Non-faith-based

Regarding non-faith-based giving, we found that Muslims give a larger proportion of their donations to overseas relief, civil rights, COVID-19, and the
environment than non-Muslims. In contrast, non-Muslims give more than
Muslims to domestic relief and health care. American Muslims provide the
largest proportion of their charity to overseas relief (18.84 percent), which is
higher than the general population which, on average, gives 12.05 percent of
its donations to this cause. This finding closely follows domestic relief (16.87
percent), which is slightly lower than the average of the general population
(19.76 percent).

American Muslims, a sizable proportion of whom are immigrants, might be
expected to spend more on their countries of origin. However, our data reveal
that Muslims also give generously to local causes. By giving to various secular
or faith-based nonprofits outside their faith tradition, American Muslims are
more likely to give to programs fighting domestic poverty than to overseas
relief.

American Muslims are also more likely than other groups to give to civil
rights organizations (11.87 percent Muslims versus 5.45 percent general
population) outside their faith community. These statistics suggest that the
experiences of discrimination may incentivize Muslims to give to their faith
communities and help other marginalized communities.

We also found that Muslim Americans gave more to COVID-19 relief
(14.26 percent), even for non-faith causes, than the average population (6.65
percent). This finding suggests that Muslims were more likely to help communities outside their faith during the COVID-19 pandemic. On the other hand,
American Muslims spend less on youth and family services (11.35 percent)
and health care (10.65 percent) outside their faith community than the general
public (12.96 percent and 13.25 percent, respectively). When coupled with
a similarly low rate of spending in this category within their faith community,
it becomes apparent that youth and family services and health care are not
a high priority for Muslims' charitable giving.

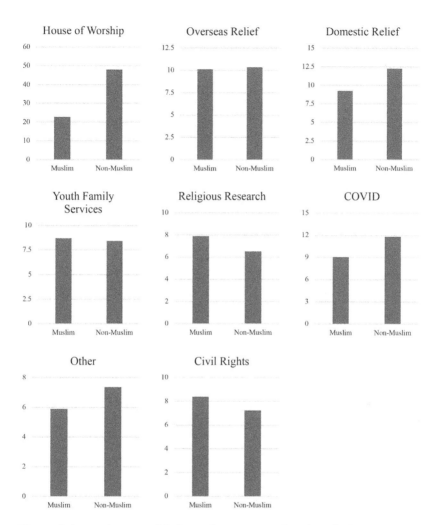

Figure 5.4   American Muslim volunteering within their faith community

Volunteering Preferences: Non-faith-based

Overall, Muslims' behavior in volunteering for non-faith-based causes is like their usual giving behavior. Muslims volunteer more hours for civil rights causes than the general population (11 percent versus 7 percent), but other than that, Muslims' volunteering behavior closely resembles that of the general population. Interestingly, the general population spends more hours volunteering for international relief causes (21 percent versus 14 percent) and domestic

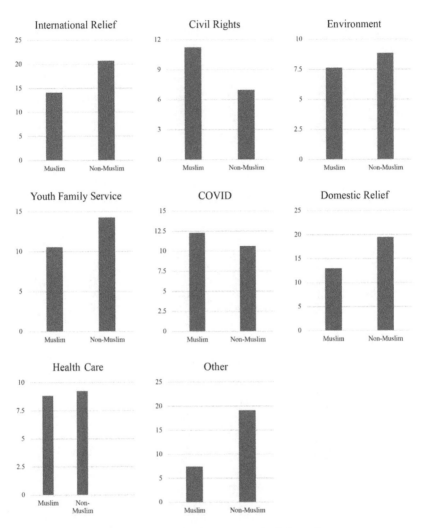

Figure 5.5   Volunteering preferences: non-faith-based

relief (19 percent versus 13 percent) than do Muslims. Again, these findings suggest that, despite many of them having immigrant backgrounds, Muslims do not overemphasize international relief at the cost of focusing on domestic causes within the United States.

Muslim Philanthropy by Gender, Age, and Race

Some interesting findings emerged about Muslim philanthropy when we looked at the data generated by the 2021 American Muslim Poll on gender, age, and race.

Gender

We found that, on average, males reported giving more than females for faith-related causes ($2,572 versus $698 for faith-based reasons and $1,984 versus $523 for non-faith causes).

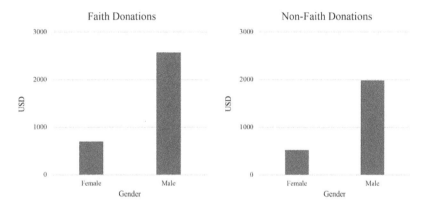

Figure 5.6   Faith and non-faith giving by gender

In terms of volunteering, we saw similar trends, as their preferences are iden-tical with regard to gender. Again, the number of hours that males volunteer is higher than that of females for both faith causes (106 versus 14 hours) and non-faith causes (65 versus 19 hours). In general, the gender priorities for causes are similar for both Muslims and non-Muslims. We found no major differences in volunteering priorities among genders except for civil rights causes. Women, on average, spend slightly more volunteering hours (13 percent versus 10 percent) on non-faith-based civil rights causes. Another main exception relates to houses of worship, where women spend more volun-teering hours than men (26 percent versus 20 percent).

Age

We found that, based on age, Muslims in the 40 to 49 age bracket have the highest average for charitable giving, whereas the lowest average for faith-based giving comes from Muslims over 50. This finding suggests that

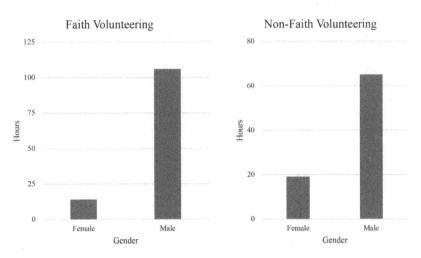

Figure 5.7   Faith and non-faith volunteering by gender

nonprofit organizations need to increase the number of younger and older people in their philanthropy efforts.

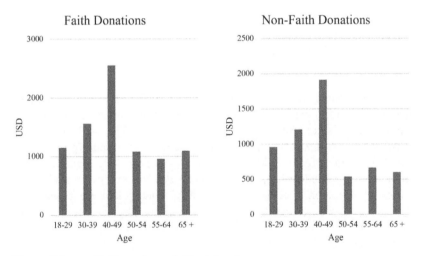

Figure 5.8   Faith and non-faith giving by age

We found similar trends in volunteering. However, one major exception is that Muslims aged 50 to 54 spend the most hours volunteering for both faith-based and non-faith-based causes. However, the amount of volunteering hours reduces after that.

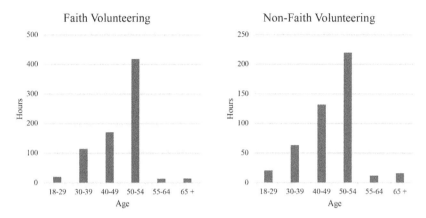

Figure 5.9   Faith and non-faith volunteering by age

Race

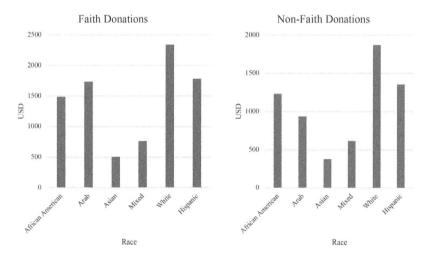

Figure 5.10   Giving by race

We found that, on average, White Muslims give the highest amounts of charity among racial groups to faith and non-faith causes. White Muslim giving is followed by that of Hispanic, Arab, African-American, Asian, and multiracial categories. We found similar results for volunteering. For instance, we found that White Muslims volunteered the most hours in 2021, followed by African-American and Hispanic Muslims.

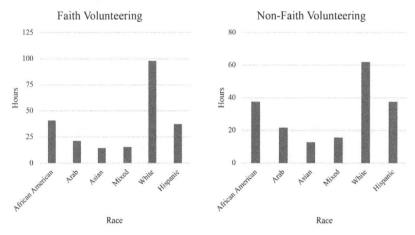

Figure 5.11   Volunteering by race

Overall, we found that the priority areas among races are similar. However, African Americans not only give the highest proportion of charity toward civil rights, both faith-based (10 percent) and non-faith-based (15 percent), but they also have the highest rate of volunteerism for civil rights causes (faith-based 24 percent and non-faith-based 11 percent).

PHILANTHROPY BEYOND NUMBERS

As we have noted, Muslims generally take a broad view of philanthropy and embrace an expansive list of actions that qualify as philanthropy. Therefore, in this survey, to measure their attitudes and for comparison purposes, we asked both the general population and the Muslim population whether they considered a broad range of practices as part of their philanthropy, including smiling, having good intentions, helping relatives, commanding right, furthering good, causing no harm, and advocating for the oppressed. We found that Muslims are significantly more likely than the general population to consider nonmonetary actions as philanthropy.

Compared with the general population, Muslims are significantly more likely ($p < 0.05$) to include smiling, good intentions, helping relatives, commanding the right actions, furthering good, not causing harm to others, and advocating for the oppressed as acts of philanthropy. Muslims are significantly and positively more likely to consider all these acts as part of their philanthropy than are non-Muslims. When controlled for religiosity and demographic covariates, these results support age, gender, education, race, and education. These findings demonstrate that Muslim Americans are more likely to believe that various nonmonetary actions are part of their philanthropy. The dataset included all the respondents in the survey (1,006 Muslim respondents and 1,004 general population respondents).

CASE STUDIES

In the following sections, we consider two modes of Muslim philanthropy taking place in the Americas, one historical and the other contemporary. The first example is that of enslaved Muslims engaging in acts of zakat and sadaqa through the freeing of other enslaved peoples, most notably in the Caribbean and in Brazil, and the giving of extemporaneous charity through baking and distributing cakes on important religious days. The second example is that of mosques and other congregational organizations (voluntary societies, mutual aid societies, coffeehouse reading groups, etc.) in the twentieth-century United States (Fahrenthold 2014, 2019; Howell 2013). Mosques and voluntary associations of Muslims coincided with increased immigration to the United States in the twentieth century (GhaneaBassiri 2010). Mosque communities served to organize new immigrants in the United States and often occurred in a parallel fashion to emergent Black Muslim traditions such as the Moorish Science Temple and the Nation of Islam. There were important convergences of these two tendencies, especially between Ahmadi Muslim missionaries and itinerant Muslim preachers working in the United States. Twentieth-century Muslim movements in the United States were acts of inclusion as well as exclusion, with many groups organizing themselves along ethnic lines, oftentimes to the exclusion of and, at times, in opposition to Black Muslim traditions.

Case Study 1: Enslaved Philanthropists

African-American Muslim philanthropy, especially sadaqa, has played and still plays an important and understudied role in American history. It is reported that nearly 15 to 20 percent of all enslaved Africans brought to North and South America as well as the Caribbean were Muslim (Turner 2013, 32). While the exact number of enslaved Africans is difficult to determine due to a lack of quantitative data—no doubt an effect of the brutal realities of the transatlantic slave trade—scholars agree that West African Muslims who were forcibly captured, sold, and brought to the Americas continued to practice Islam in various ways, often covertly. Importantly, there are several well-documented accounts of enslaved Muslims writing in Arabic, praying, fasting, and continuing to engage in practices of charity despite the inhospitable conditions and, at times, forced conversions of enslaved peoples to Christianity. The recorded lives and experiences of Salih Bilali, Ayyuba Suleyman Diallo, Abd al-Rahman Ibrahima, Omar ibn Said, and others attest to the presence of Muslims who were trained and educated in the West African Islamic scholarly traditions and continued that practice in America (Curtis 2009; Diouf 2013; GhaneaBassiri 2010; Gomez 2005; Hammer and Safi 2013).

The study of enslaved African Muslim practices of charity is one reason why an expanded definition of philanthropy is necessary. Enslaved Africans did not practice what we consider formal philanthropy today, that is, institutionalized voluntary giving of time and money; yet they engaged in activities that not only aided others but also sustained a sense of community under inhumane conditions. As mentioned in a previous chapter, one of the eight causes to which one gives zakat includes the freeing of enslaved peoples. Sylviane Diouf (2022) argued that societies of formerly enslaved peoples and so-called "slave revolts" in Trinidad and Brazil should be understood through the lens of Muslim philanthropy, namely as acts of zakat (25–8). Diouf also stated that "long before the Emancipation Proclamation in 1834, Trinidad had a free Muslim community whose members belonged to an association known variously as the Free Mandingo of Trinidad, the Mandingo Society, and the Free Mohammedans" (25). Moreover, these free Muslims organized themselves and pooled resources in a common fund that they used "to redeem their coreligionists, including those who had just arrived. When a slave ship landed, they went on board and redeemed the Muslims" (26).

In addition to freeing of enslaved peoples, Muslims in Brazil also gave zakat al-fitr, a special form of zakat given during the month of Ramadan to those in need so that they are not forced to beg openly. While not mentioned in the Qur'an, this practice is conveyed in various narrations of the Prophet Muhammad, called hadith. There are minor differences in opinion on when and how zakat al-fitr should be paid and for whom it is obligatory according to various schools of Islamic jurisprudence, but all are in agreement that it is obligatory (Zysow 2012). This form of zakat is usually paid in the form of foodstuffs, clothing, or shelter. Diouf (2013) notes that in Brazil, Muslims would give saka (rice cakes) at the end of Ramadan to those in need and in this way fulfilled their requirement to pay zakat al-fitr to support the less fortunate (92).

The largest concentration of enslaved Muslims was in Georgia and South Carolina. Through oral histories and recorded traditions passed down by the descendants of enslaved African Muslims, scholars have been able to reconstruct a general picture of early Muslim philanthropy in the United States. There is a long-standing tradition of West African Muslim women baking sweet rice cakes and distributing them on Fridays as a form of alms. Enslaved

Muslim women would make sweet rice cakes to distribute to enslaved children every Friday and on "a big day" every year, which would most likely be the Eid celebrations following the end of Ramadan. Children would say the Arabic word "Ameen" three times and then eat the cakes. One can only imagine what these sweet white balls meant to those enslaved children. Many of the children were separated, through sale, from their families, lived in oppressive conditions, and were expected to work to produce profit for the plantation owners. These cakes were known as "saraka," which is a common West African linguistic alteration of the word sadaqa. This act of cooking sarakas and distributing them monthly or annually was an act of sadaqa through which enslaved Muslims continued to practice their faith traditions.

Enslaved Muslim Americans were active in practicing their faith and embraced charitable donations as an important tool in other ways. Another enslaved Muslim American, Prince Abdul Rahman, and his wife came to the North to raise funds to purchase the freedom of his children who remained in slavery after he was recognized as being emancipated from slavery. Due to hatred of Islam, he was presented as a convert to Christianity (GhaneaBassiri 2012). In both of these cases, Muslims were seeking to find solutions to problems beyond Islamic obligatory giving of zakat. In the case of the enslaved women, it was to think of ways they could make the lives of others better and using nonmonetary resources to do so. In the case of Prince Abdul Rahman, it was to use his voice and his narrative to help free his enslaved children using funds from non-Muslims.

Case Study 2: Mosque Philanthropy

Mosques are another important element of Muslim-American philanthropic practice. According to a recent study, giving to mosques is one of highest priorities for giving within the faith (Siddiqui and Wasif 2021). These houses of worship contribute by preaching the teachings of Islam, offering community-building and appealing for contributions to help the needy. Chronological records maintain that mosques existed in America as early as 1925, but only 2 percent of modern mosques were established prior to 1950. The first continuing mosque in America was built in Cedar Rapids, Iowa, in 1920 in a rented hall and was completed in 1934. However, in 1914 an Islamic Center was established, and in 1924 it became the Modern Age Arabian Islamic Society. In Ross, North Dakota, Muslims established a mosque in 1920 but had to abandon it later. The first mosque in New York was established in the 1930s by immigrants from Poland, Russia, and Lithuania; the second mosque called the Islamic Mission of America was also established in the 1930s by a Moroccan immigrant. The earliest mosque in Michigan was established in 1919 in Dearborn but had a very short lifespan. However, when the

Ford Motor Company established a plant in Dearborn, the Arab-Muslim community there thrived and built a Sunni mosque in 1938 and a Shi'i mosque in 1940. Seven, primarily Lebanese, families who settled in the Boston area in the early 1900s worked to establish a mosque that was finally completed in 1963 (Bagby, Perl, and Froehle 2001; GhaneaBassiri 2010; Hammer and Safi 2013).

The US Mosque Survey, conducted in 2020, found that at that time there were 2,769 mosques (with over 2,000 of them built after 9/11/2001), an increase of 31 percent from 2010. This increase is the result of the growing Muslim population due to both immigration and an increasing birth rate (Bagby 2021). Muslim scholars argue that building mosques does not qualify for zakat funding. However, mosques have become a vital part of Muslim life in the United States.

Mosques are also catalysts and incubators of sadaqa and are important parts of philanthropy among American Muslims. Eighty-four percent of mosques are reported to give cash assistance to families or individuals; 74 percent provide counseling services; 60 percent have prison or jail programs; 55 percent have a food pantry, soup kitchen, or collect food for the poor; 53 percent have a thrift store or collect clothes for the poor; 28 percent have a tutoring or literacy program; 18 percent have an anti-drug or anti-crime program; 16 percent have a daycare or pre-school program; and 12 percent have a substance abuse program (Bagby et al. 2001).

CONCLUSION

This chapter focused on the Muslim practice of sadaqa by examining the philanthropic practices of Muslim-American giving. The results show that the practice of sadaqa is highly prevalent in Muslim societies and that it takes multiple forms, both formal and informal. We find that Muslims are significantly more willing to embrace a broader definition of philanthropy than the general population.

In terms of monetary giving and volunteering, our findings show that Muslims are more generous than the general population. In fact, in 2021, Muslims gave an estimated $4.4 million in zakat. We also find that Muslims are more likely to consider acts of service as part of their philanthropy, from minor acts (e.g., having good intentions and smiling) to more prominent displays of charitable actions (e.g., volunteerism and advocating for the oppressed), and embrace the idea that sadaqa does not mean only monetary giving but that individuals can give according to their means—even during the harshest times, including the time of slavery when the earliest Muslim Americans partook in sadaqa through acts such as baking cakes for children. These findings highlight the importance of thinking beyond numbers when considering philanthropy and understanding philanthropic practices beyond Western-centric definitions.

These findings have multiple implications. First, they provide context for how Muslim Americans might practice philanthropy. They also speak to how Muslim Americans understand the scope and meaning of philanthropy. Research shows that individuals—especially those with nondominant religious and cultural traditions—understand that the practice of philanthropy is crucial to fostering increased recognition, understanding, and inclusion of diverse forms of philanthropy. Overall, the findings from this study can broaden our knowledge of philanthropy from the perspective of a minority, faith-based community, as well as highlight informal forms of philanthropy, which can be challenging to measure and capture.

NOTE

1. This estimate is based on the assumption that the average Muslim household of four in an average population is spending an average of $1,810 (USD) on faith-based causes and $1,138 on non-faith-based causes.

6.   The waqf: evolution of an institution

Abu Hurairah, may Allah be pleased with him, narrated that the Messenger of Allah
(ﷺ) said: "When a person dies, his deeds are cut off except for three:
Continuing charity, knowledge that others benefited from, and a righteous son who
supplicates for him."
Hadith of the Prophet Muhammad (al-Tirmidhi n.d.)

Perhaps no term better exemplifies the practice of Islamic charity than the word
"waqf" (plural awqaf), often translated as "pious or charitable endowment,"
and sometimes as foundation or trust. Historically, a waqf was an endowed
immovable asset (typically property) given to God and dedicated via deed
for a specific charitable purpose. The waqf is a dynamic institution created
for both community welfare and private beneficiaries, especially the family
or offspring of the founder (Ghazaleh 2011). Mosques, hospitals, educational
institutions, public fountains, and soup kitchens were all the result of charitable endowments given by wealthy Muslims, both men and women,[1] who
dedicated the use (i.e., the usufruct) of their property for public benefit and
contractually passed the ownership of the property to God. While technically
"God's property," the administration of the waqf often remained in the hands
of the endower's family and could be passed down through generations as
stipulated in the endowment deed. Historian Mariam Hoexter summarized the
institution of the waqf in the following way: "The basic idea of the endowment
as a continuous or eternal charity is reflected in the definition that appears in
virtually every waqf manual: *al-waqf sadaqa jariya fi sabil Allah ta`ala*—the
waqf is a continuous charity for the sake of God and his religion" (2002, 122).

As the practice of endowing waqfs developed, these institutions grew more
complex. In the early modern period (fifteenth through seventeenth centuries), scholars in the Ottoman Empire developed and enlarged the practice of
endowing money, called cash waqfs, which resulted in greater mobility since
the endowed assets were no longer restricted in practice to immovables (Saiti,
Dembele, and Bulut 2021, 278). As European empires expanded into Africa,
Eastern Europe, the Middle East, and South and Southeast Asia, colonial
administrators sought to repurpose the waqf to open up rich waqf lands to
the predations of capital and trade (Powers 1989). The social, political, and
economic transformations of the colonial nineteenth and twentieth centuries
placed the waqf at the center of debates about religion, the family, and the
economy. As a result, Muslim scholars, political reformers, and state admin-

istrators sought to regulate the waqf through the creation of bureaucratic institutions.

Over the past half-century, various governments and development agencies across the globe have refocused their attention on waqfs, especially cash waqfs, as a potential catalyst for social change and development, specifically poverty alleviation on national and international scales (Saiti et al. 2021, 279). Moreover, Muslim NGOs, international organizations, and scholars have advocated the use of waqf as a shariʿa-compliant form of investment pooling in order to combat socioeconomic problems in Muslim-majority states as well as nations with sizeable Muslim minorities such as India (Sachar Committee Report 2006). For instance, the World Bank claims that waqfs are "a potent tool for mobilizing resources to meet societal needs by the self-sustaining contributions of private donors rather than by governmental borrowing or spending of tax money" (Abdul Aziz et al. 2019). In this way, waqf development has emerged as a part of a global conversation regarding solutions to the decline or absence of the welfare state in addition to advancing the United Nation's Sustainable Development Goals (SDGs) (Abdullah 2018). The use of waqfs as instruments of international development projects marks a shift in their use from being a tool to support the poor to being a mechanism for the elimination of poverty: "The discussions on waqf are aligned with the World Bank's twin goals to end extreme poverty and promote shared prosperity in every country sustainably" (Abdul Aziz et al. 2019).

However, despite the increasing salience of the waqf in finance, development, and nonprofit sectors, there is still disagreement in the scholarship of philanthropy about whether waqfs represent an alternative financial instrument for Muslim development or whether the waqf is analogous to an endowment, trust, or foundation. For instance, the World Bank defines waqfs as a type of private charity administered by "private managers" (Abdul Aziz et al. 2019). On the other hand, USAID describes the waqf as a foundation (Alterman, Hunter, and Phillips 2005). Others consider waqfs a form of trust, although differences exist between the development of trust law and the legal operations of waqfs (Akhtar 2013; Adam 2020; Schoenblum 1999).

In this chapter, we provide an overview of how waqfs were developed as a socioeconomic tool of piety and prestige aimed at public benefit by examining their role historically and their development, transformation, and repurposing in the present. Moreover, we focus our analysis of Muslim philanthropy within the context of the United States to show how this historically significant institution was adapted to the social, legal, and political context of American philanthropy.

HISTORICAL INTRODUCTION

The etymology of the word "waqf" is an instructive point to begin our overview of the practice of endowing assets, most often property but also cash, *in perpetuity* for the sake of God. Derived from the Arabic trilateral root w-q-f (waqafa, or ف ق), its literal meaning is "to stop" or "to hold" (Abbasi 2012, 124). In the case of the waqf as a charitable institution, waqf refers to the detention of property from circulation via sale, inheritance, gift, or other forms of alienation (Dallal 2004, 17). Historically, this property, dedicated to God and forbidden from passing into the ownership of a third party, must be used for the stated purpose outlined in its founding deed, called a waqfiyya (Abbasi 2012; Dallal 2004). While not explicitly found in the Qur'an, the first and most authoritative source of Islamic jurisprudence, the earliest account of the institution that would come to be known as waqf dates back to the time of the Prophet Muhammad and the initial community of believers in the seventh century (Gil 1998; Schacht 1953). The historian Ahmed Dallal (2004) recounts one of the earliest prophetic precedents for the creation of the waqf, known at the time as habs (plural: hubus, a term still used in North Africa) or sadaqa mawqufa:

> [U]pon his request, 'Umar (a companion of the Prophet and the second caliph of Islam) is advised by Muhammad to "retain the corpus [of the land of Thamgh, in the region of Khaybar] but dedicate its fruits [in the way of] God." According to this tradition, 'Umar dedicated the land indicating that it should not be sold, given away as a gift, or inherited. He also stipulated that the revenue from the land be used as charity for the poor, for his relatives, for setting slaves free, for wanderers, and for other social needs. (2004, 15)

Historical accounts in which Muslims are encouraged to engage in acts of perpetual charity (sadaqa jariya) in the path of God (fi sabil Allah), which we see in the example above, can be found in several sources such as prophetic biographies, collections of prophetic traditions (hadith), and Islamic jurisprudential texts (fiqh). These sources attest to the early significance of the institution of the waqf, which was further enlarged and developed as a mechanism of Islamic charity (both public and private)[2] via jurisprudential debates in the ninth and tenth centuries (Gil 1998; Hennigan 2004; Oberauer 2013). Legal historian Peter Hennigan (2004) argued that these later jurisprudential debates "gave birth to the legal institution" of the waqf, which systematized and legitimated the legal terminology of the waqf for subsequent generations of scholars (2004, 50–52). While the origins and early formation of waqfs have been subject to debate among historians of Islam, it is undeniable that the institution has been readily adopted by Muslims from North Africa and Eastern Europe to Central and Southeast Asia.

Public Goods and Private Benefits

Waqfs have several charitable purposes and therefore can be divided into two broad categories: the public good waqf (waqf khayri) and the family waqf (waqf ahli) (Shatzmiller 2001, 46). Legally, these two institutions were identical, only to be differentiated by their stated purpose. Public good waqfs were to be used for a specified public benefit, while family waqfs were endowed to "aid the founder's kin and descendants" (McChesney 1991, 1182:9). R. D. McChesney (1991), a historian of Central Asia, noted that these two categories of waqf were not exclusive and could, at times, be mixed:

> In many cases ... the foundation served both purposes simultaneously ... benefiting family members and supporting a public institution. Such waqf deeds might specify that family members would receive a certain percentage of the income either as foundation officials or as direct beneficiaries, while the remainder would be used to maintain a public institution. (1991, 1182:9)

Importantly, the preservation of lineage and the benefit of the Muslim community are included as necessary "objectives of the shari'a" (maqasid al-shari'a), a juristic tool and methodology used to discern the scope and justification of Islamic legal norms (Duderija 2014), both of which are central to the justification of the waqf as an institution of Muslim communities. While the preservation of lineage and community benefit are legible to modern legal and charitable structures, the waqf also secured the possibility for the continued practice of "Islamic ways of life," through sustaining mosques, schools, shrines, and other sites of pilgrimage and worship across the world (Moumtaz 2021, 38).

The public good waqf entailed the owner of an asset (e.g., property) passing that ownership to God and dedicating the benefits (menfa'a) of that asset (e.g., rent) to a charitable purpose according to the stipulations laid out in a deed. As scholars have recently pointed out, this charitable purpose was broad in scope and included one's own family as an object of charity (Dallal 2004, 22; Moumtaz 2018). Historian Eyal Ginio (1997) stated, "the institution of the family endowment, which allows the founder to specify the identity of the future beneficiaries of his endowment, to include as beneficiaries individuals who are not legal heirs, and to exclude others who are" (1997, 390). Importantly, this also included manumitted slaves under certain conditions in which no eligible heirs or the founder remained childless (Shaham 2000). Since inheritance laws were strictly delineated in both the Qur'an and the Islamic legal tradition, waqfs provided a means to support offspring and extended kinship networks in addition to other dependents who would likely be passed over in the disbursement of inheritance.

Prior to the modern period, most public goods were provided by private individuals or groups rather than by state governments (Kuran 2001, 842). In this system, hospitals, schools, food pantries, animal shelters, soup kitchens, and the like were private initiatives. In Muslim-majority and -minority societies, these services were provided through the waqf. Waqfs were central to the socioeconomic fabric of pre- and early modern societies; Mehmet Bulut and Cem Korkut (2019) went so far as to say that the Ottoman Empire was a "waqf civilization" in which "all public services were funded with income from the waqfs and the continuity of services was ensured with this regular income" (2019, 98, 101), forming what they consider to be an alternative financial system and worldview. Importantly, waqfs were not used solely by Muslims, as non-Muslims with financial means also availed themselves to the waqf for both public charitable purposes—often for the support of a particular religious community or cause—and for creating family endowments (Shaham 1991). Increasingly in the nineteenth century, imperial polities sought to regulate and centralize these private initiatives, giving greater control to government bureaucracies in an attempt to oversee the workings and management of such vast waqf properties and endowments (Çizakça 2000; Moumtaz 2021, 79–110).

A third category of waqf deserves mention but is beyond the scope of this chapter, that is, the imperial waqf, established by "sultans, dynasty members, and high-ranking state servants," notably under the dynastic rule of the Ottomans (Orbay 2017, 135). These waqfs performed several purposes such as endowing large-scale educational institutions and houses of worship in addition to preserving wealth from confiscation by appointing family members as administrators (Orbay 2017, 139).

These grand, imperial waqfs are often what modern waqf advocates have in mind when they think back to earlier historical periods as exemplary models of private Muslim beneficence and civilizational advancement. However, in this chapter, we focus on the public good or charitable waqf, with some attention paid to the family waqf to inquire into the various charitable institutional mechanisms that Muslims have developed and how they are being discussed and utilized today. Additionally, we ask whether modern "family foundations" established by Muslims in the United States could be considered an adaptation or translation of the family waqf under different legal and civic formations. We turn to that question at the end of this chapter.

However, the waqf is not without its modern critics and skeptics as well. Timur Kuran (2001), an economist and critic of the waqf system, claimed that the waqf was a means to circumvent restrictive inheritance laws detailed in the Qur'an and specified in various schools of jurisprudence. He stated that "the waqf system served ... as a credible commitment device aimed at providing the owners of land and other immovable assets economic security in return for investments in public goods. The system thus promoted social services by providing their suppliers protections against revenue-seeking rulers" (2001, 843). While the waqf served as a flexible institution of the medieval and early modern Muslim world, by the nineteenth century Kuran (2001) argued that its legal structure became an obstacle to its growth as an "enterprise enjoying corporate status" (2001, 843). Kuran further suggested that the waqf failed to sufficiently cultivate a robust civil society because it was overly constrained by "the force of law" (2001, 881), despite allowing for the autonomous organization of private capital for public benefit. Ultimately, Kuran claimed that what was once a vibrant institution of Islamic social and economic life became a deterrent, keeping Muslim societies from developing robust civil society instruments—a strong claim that has been met with much criticism from Muslim and non-Muslim scholars alike (2001, 844).[3]

For Kuran, the waqf served as an instrument with two contradictory aims. The first was the continued material security of the founder's wealth, which could be maintained and administered by whomever he or she named in their deed as administrator of waqf with a strict emphasis on the founder's explicitly stated intentions. The second was the provision of public good (khayr, literally goodness), especially for the poor and students, but also for the benefit of the local community at large. Kuran's thesis is that the rigidity of the former ultimately reduced the capacity of the latter to meet changing needs, especially under different political conditions. In this framing, the culprit behind "underdevelopment" is neither colonialism nor imperial debt structures, but a strict adherence to the letter of Islamic law, which was insufficiently flexible. Economic historian Murat Çizakça has taken issue with Kuran's thesis, arguing that it relies largely on conjecture with little comparative historical data to demonstrate that Islamic law was at fault. Çizakça (2011) insisted that the Islamic legal and economic system was indeed flexible; reasons for "underdevelopment" cannot be reduced to Islamic legal principles, but must take into consideration various external, material factors such as the following: "geography, price and profit controls, high rates of interest (twice the permitted rates of profit), property rights restrictions, widespread confiscations and sustained crowding-out effect" (2011, 118). What Kuran attributed to ideological causes (theological and legal restrictions), Çizakça claimed are due to modern material, social, and political forces shaping Muslim societies (Crow 2013).

Waqf in the Modern World System

European orientalists (scholars specializing in the study of so-called "Eastern" or "Oriental" traditions) and colonial officials wrote extensively on the socio-economic institutions of Muslim life (J. N. D. Anderson 1951; 1952). Due to the imperial nature of European interests in Muslim-majority and -minority regions of Africa, the Middle East, and South and Southeast Asia, institutions of socioeconomic significance fell under colonial governments' legal and political influence (J. N. D. Anderson 1959). While the British allowed for personal status laws to remain under the control of the indigenous authority in the territories they administered, anything relating to commercial practice fell under British commercial law and regulations to facilitate trade across the Empire (Hofri-Winogradow 2012, 815–17). Given the waqf's important economic place in Muslim civil society, it was no exception and came under intensified scrutiny by imperial governments (French, British, Dutch, etc.) as well as regional powers (e.g., Ottoman) that sought centralized control and management (Abbasi 2014; Oberauer 2008; Macnaghten 1897; Hoexter 1998).

For example, David Powers (1989) demonstrated how, "the [French] colonial administration endeavored to gain control over the endowment institution through a series of legislative enactments and was assisted by French orientalists who campaigned to discredit the institution among the Algerians themselves" (1989, 536). This act of discrediting was important for colonial governments and imperial powers because, as Barnes (1987, 43–4) has estimated, by the nineteenth century nearly two-thirds of property in territories such as the Ottoman Empire was held as waqfs and, thus, restricted from certain capital market pressures and forces (Powers 1989, 537).

Waqf and Civil Society

Scholars from a number of fields have suggested that the waqf was key to Muslim civil society and public services prior to the rise of the modern welfare state (Hoexter 2002). For example, the political theorist Engin F. Isin (2011) argued that in the seventeenth and eighteenth centuries, the Ottoman waqf formed the basis of a broader, non-republican notion of citizenship: "When we consider citizenship not as contract or status but as acts and practices that enable subjects to negotiate differences, we find that the waqf ... [was] indeed [a] sophisticated act of citizenship" (2011, 224). The waqf was not a juristic person in the way the medieval church or early modern corporation was, but as Isin and Lefebvre (2005) claimed, it "endow[ed] the subject with qualities of citizenship, which is to say autonomy, right, and legal recourse" (2005, 14). This more expansive understanding of the waqf and its role in Muslim history allows us to move beyond the tired dichotomy of economic development versus religious fidelity and observe how an unmistakably "religious" institution performed important activities for cultivating civil society.

Despite the importance of the waqf as an institution of civil society, the literature on nonprofits and development has yet to extensively address the dynamic role of waqfs as an instrument of philanthropic practice. Another body of scholarship discusses waqfs as a form of charitable institutions in the

Islamic tradition (Petersen 2012; Einolf 2017; Godfrey, Branigan, and Khan 2017; Salamon and Anheier 1992). For example, Wang and Li (2022) discussed the prevalence of waqf institutions for Muslims in China, and Godfrey, Branigan, and Khan (2017) focused on the institution of waqf in India during the Mughal Empire. However, due to the legal technicalities of the waqf and the historical and legal specializations needed to analyze the relevant literature, scholars in the field of nonprofit studies have yet to fully engage the historical development and transformations of waqfs and, instead, speak of them generally in the context of Muslim philanthropy or as instruments to be levied in development projects and financial investment. In this vein, Kaleem and Ahmed (2010) proposed using money raised from waqf funds to fund microfinance institutions in the Muslim world. Thus, a majority of the nonprofit scholarship on Islamic philanthropy has considered the waqf to be a form of the foundation, perhaps even its precursor, belonging to Muslim societies (Jung, Harrow, and Leat 2018). Yet there has been little discussion of the different genealogies of foundations in Euro-American and Muslim traditions, with few exceptions (Çizakça 2000; Adam 2020; Falus 2020).

So, is the waqf a foundation or an endowment? Thomas Adam (2020, 58) argued that the crucial difference between the two is that an endowment is given to an existing legal entity while the foundation creates a new one. In the historical context of Western Europe, endowments were usually given to the Christian church or monastic orders and used accordingly. Perhaps more interesting is the argument by Herrold (2018), who claimed, based on extensive research in Egypt and Palestine, that waqfs now closely resemble private foundations where a single donor and a board make decisions on behalf of the donor. The modern waqf resembles the institutions of the foundation, endowment, and trust and has evolved to mirror these forms due to the global adoption of modern legal codes and governance structures of the contemporary nation-state. In a fascinating reversal of historical transfer, some scholars have claimed that the endowment was originally based on and adapted from the Islamic waqf, as in the case of Merton College at Oxford (Makdisi 1981; Gaudiosi 1988); yet the contemporary waqf now draws from the example of the Euro-American foundation and endowment as a model for its revival. An example of the resemblance between the contemporary foundation and the waqf is the adoption of waqf boards to administer and manage the endowment instead of a single individual. Historically, the administrator of the waqf was called a mutawalli and was directly appointed by the founder. Importantly, this change involves an act of *translation* rather than a simple act of adopting a modern legal term for a long-existing Islamic institution. In the case of waqfs in the United States, many Muslim founders and boards have invoked the concept of the waqf when establishing a foundation. Ultimately, these foundations have brought together the community foundation practice of raising funds from various community members with the waqf practice of using endowed funds for community development while reserving the principle.

M. Z. Abbasi (2012) stated that across a majority of Islamic legal traditions, "the family of the founder is also given preference in the appointment of the *mutawalli* (administrator) by the *qadi* [judge] who should appoint one from the family of the founder where no one is specified and the post falls vacant" (2012, 127). However, unlike modern-day nonprofits or private foundations, which are governed by a board vested with certain powers and privileges such as amending or altering bylaws, the mutawalli was obliged to act according to the waqf deed (waqfiyya), and any changes that required amending or altering the aim or purpose of the waqf were done following the procedural rules of an Islamic legal school and decided by a judge (qadi). In this sense, it is difficult to say that a waqf is *structurally* the same as an endowment, foundation, or trust, because unlike these legal entities, a waqf's operation and governance was dependent on a long tradition of Islamic theological and legal practice, which required Islamic scholarly expertise. However, as noted above, the organization of the waqf form has taken on attributes of foundations and endowments as they were reimagined in the colonial transformation of the modern state.

Notwithstanding these standard features, Kuran (2016) draws an important distinction between the traditional and the modern form of waqf. The former prohibited resource pooling and mandated strict uses of the endowment as stipulated by the founder. These institutional rigidities are at the heart of Kuran's original thesis that the waqf historically stymied innovation and growth across the Middle East. However, more recent manifestations of the institution across the Muslim world appear more flexible than their historical counterpart. The now-pervasive modern waqf looks more akin to a charitable foundation that allows for institutional growth and change beyond the original founder's directive, while still restricting the use of waqf assets to activities with a religious purpose. To quote Kuran (2016), the modern waqf "has managerial flexibilities denied to its Islamic namesake," "is directed by a board of trustees rather than a single caretaker," "may invest in liquid assets," and "can engage in politics" even "in cooperation with other entities, including other waqf" (2016, 445).

WAQF AS SOCIAL WELFARE?

Over the course of the twentieth century, Muslim scholars, community members, investors, and nonprofit and NGO leaders have turned to the waqf as a model of Muslim civil society and tool for "social development," that is, a mechanism of welfare redistribution aimed at remedying global inequalities, especially those affecting Muslim-majority societies as well as Muslim minorities (Ali, Hassan, and Ali 2019, 1:4–5). Others, such as Zara Khan

(2021) believe modern waqfs can be repurposed to address poverty, income inequality, and other forms of "structural injustice." As legal historian Sabrina Joseph (2014, 425–6) noted, "Referring to pre-nineteenth-century examples of the role of waqf in society, modern day thinkers articulate that waqf, with the proper legal mechanisms in place, has the potential to foster civil society, reduce the financial burden on states by providing social services at the community level and act as a vehicle for the promotion of sustainability" (425–6).

While historically the asset given to God for perpetual charity was immovable as in the case of real estate, it has become increasingly common for the waqf to be based in movable assets such as cash. Yet the cash waqf is a familiar institution. It has been in continuous use since the fifteenth and sixteenth centuries when Ottoman legal scholars engaged in jurisprudential debates argued for the permissibility of cash for using waqf under limitations imposed by shariʿa principles. These early modern scholars returned to previous legal debates to ground their arguments for endowing movable property (cash), whose value was subject to fluctuation based on the market and the nature of the investments (Mandaville 1979, 293–5).

Hassan, Karim, and Karim (2019) contended that cash waqfs are no different from property-based assets in that property is also subject to depreciation, especially in the case of climate-induced transformations (e.g., river erosion of waqf lands in Bangladesh). Since all things are perishable in an ultimate sense, these scholars argued, the typical objections to cash waqf—that they are movable and perishable—no longer hold the same weight. As long as the corpus is maintained, invested in a shariʿa-compliant manner, and given to acceptable charitable purposes, it is a permissible form of charity (2019, 61). Furthermore, they asserted that the benefits of the cash waqf outweigh the risks; the cash waqf can immediately generate income, it is affordable, requires minimal maintenance and development, and allows Muslims without real estate assets to participate by donating and pooling cash (2019, 61).

Yet imagining the modern waqf as an institution of social welfare and a tool for social development requires the work of *conceptual translation*. The waqf is a legal institution with a deep history and is inextricably connected to interpretive questions rooted in theological, legal, ethical, and economic discourses. Complicating matters further, modern waqfs are often established and maintained under secular legal regimes and are subject to global financial forces and practices that might be at odds with principles of Islamic finance, such as high-risk, speculative investments or interest-bearing loans. Furthermore, scholars such as Habib Ahmed (2019) have argued that there are "major impediments" to the development of waqfs due to "discriminatory legal treatment of these institutions compared to other non-profits" (2019, 154).

Scholars and practitioners seeking to translate Muslim charitable practices into contemporary developmental and financial institutions and instruments have aimed to reimagine the waqf as a mechanism for achieving Sustainable Development Goals (SDGs). More interesting, perhaps, is their effort to translate SDGs via the concept of maqasid al-shari'a, or the aims of the shari'a, which include the preservation of religion, life, intelligence, progeny, and wealth (Ibrahim and Khan 2019, 232). Scholars have argued that since these objectives are commensurate with the United Nations' SDGs, then Muslim social development tools like the waqf "can play an intermediary role in actualising mutual targets of both the SDGs and the maqasid al-shariah" (Abdullah 2018, 159). Abdullah and others actually extend this claim into the past by arguing that waqf as a social welfare tool is not simply a charitable institution commensurate with global development frameworks like SDGs, but that the waqf actually aimed at achieving these goals prior to their articulation as such (2018, 159).

WAQF AS FOUNDATION IN AMERICA

Thus far, we have provided a detailed historical introduction to the waqf, its transformation in the modern period, and some of the major debates on the topic. The following five case studies provide us with different pathways that Muslims in the United States have taken in practicing the Islamic tradition of waqf in a contemporary context. As we have stated, Muslims in the United States are highly diverse; therefore, no one model can accurately describe their approach to bringing this Islamic practice to life in the contemporary context. Interestingly, only one of these institutions uses the term waqf in its title. The remaining institutions have found existing generic American terms to describe their work. Due to Islamophobia and external scrutiny, Muslims have long sought to describe their institutions using terms that would be easily understood by an external audience with the belief that the institution's work would speak for itself with an internal audience. For example, many Islamic centers in the 1980s and 1990s described themselves as an "Islamic or Muslim society" or as an "Islamic or Muslim community center," versus masjid or mosque. This approach brings external and internal legitimacy (Siddiqui 2013). Assuring donors, members, and supporters that the work being undertaken in establishing an institution complies with US law provides a needed assurance to a highly scrutinized and racialized community.

This has changed over time. After 2001, Muslims in the United States started testing ways in which their religious and civic identity would be accepted by a broader community. In 2009, President Obama created important civic opportunities for Muslim leaders. However, after President Trump's election, those who opposed him largely embraced Muslims in the United States. Therefore, it is not surprising that Islamic Relief USA, a successful national charity that is broadly accepted by Muslims, the government, and interfaith partners, would embrace the term waqf in the title of its new endowment.

The North American Islamic Trust (NAIT) is among the first institutional establishments presented in the following case studies. NAIT was established as a supporting, yet independent, institution for the Muslim Student Association of North America (MSA) and later the Islamic Society of North America (ISNA). Established to protect assets while creating revenue opportunities to further the work of MSA and later ISNA, it operated as a traditional waqf would by safeguarding community assets (property) and creating new businesses (bookstores and a printing press). It later expanded its efforts by investing endowment funds through the stock market and then established its own mutual fund. Arguably, the investments in non-real estate or non-tangible businesses would be a divergence from traditional waqf models.

The El-Hibri Foundation was established in the aftermath of the terrorist attacks on September 11, 2001. It was an attempt by a devout Muslim to further his religious values and was also an attempt to give an external audience a tangible example of Muslim contributions to the United States, as one of the first foundations of its kind with a staff, a presence in Washington, DC, and a traditional grant program.

Islamic Relief USA Waqf was established in 2012 as a traditional religious endowment for Islamic Relief USA while also serving as a symbol to revive the tradition of the waqf. It was the actions of a highly successful and confident institution that embraced its legitimacy as an exceptionally successful charity as well as an established Islamic organization.

The American Muslim Community Foundation was founded in 2016 in an attempt not only to establish one of the first Muslim community foundations but also to harness the community opportunities of the cash waqf model that was established in the late Ottoman period. Perhaps the complexity and disagreement of the cash waqf model and the need to embrace an American legal form led to the embrace of the community foundation, versus the cash waqf terminology. What follows are five case studies of American Muslim organizations that model themselves after the tradition of waqf.

North American Islamic Trust

On May 23, 1973, the North American Islamic Trust (NAIT) was incorporated in the state of Indiana to serve "the bests interests of Islam and the Muslim Students Association of the US & Canada [MSA]."[4] At its inceptions, it stated that it had $3,040,000 in assets, which included property in Gary, Indiana and Ann Arbor, Michigan; a printing press in Maryland; and the Islamic Book Service in Cincinnati. Apart from an initial declaration to serve the best interest of MSA, there was little other reference to Islam (in its founding documents).

However, across 18 subparagraphs, the founders of NAIT detailed an organization that would own property, acquire funds, reinvest, and distribute income to further its broader purpose. It was established by members of the MSA, including Dr. Jamal Barzinji, Dr. Ahmad Sakr, Dr. Moinuddin Siddiqui, and Osman Ahmad, all of whom were key leaders in MSA and later in the Islamic Society of North America (ISNA). It was not until December 15, 2014, that the NAIT board formally identified the Islamic term "waqf" as the appropriate descriptor for the 18 activities it described in its founding documents.[5] Since its founding in 1973, NAIT has become one of the largest community endowments in North America and includes more than 300 properties (mostly Islamic centers or schools), an Islamic mutual fund, an endowment fund for Muslim organizations, and an important loan program that funds completion of mosque or Islamic school projects.[6] In 2022, NAIT distilled its purpose down to four simple objectives:

- Revive Prophet's Sunnah of Waqf
- Shield Islamic centers' properties from potential legal liabilities
- Pool Muslim American communities' financial assets for mutual gains
- Offer shariʿa-compliant financial products

By 2021, it had over $156 million assets under management through its mutual fund. To understand NAIT today, it is critical that we examine MSA and ISNA and their precursors, the Federation of Islamic Associations of North America and Canada (FIA). These two organizations have a connected history that illustrates how a group of Muslims in the United States sought to institutionalize Islamic institutions in the United States.

Federation of Islamic Associations of North America and Canada

Muslim-American veterans founded FIA in the aftermath of World War II. These founders were largely Arab Americans born in the United States. They sought to engage a more diverse Muslim-American population in order to unify this populace. During this time, FIA became an effective and politically engaged entity (Howell 2010). In its attempt to bridge the divide between Muslims who were religious or secular, it needed to balance its activities. For instance, it annually hosted formal banquets featuring live entertainment and less formal sock hops and other youth dances. At the same time, FIA hosted events that focused on religious education.

By the 1970s, FIA had become increasingly divided between those who valued the organization's ethnic roots and social agenda and those who thought it should become a strictly religious organization. The founders of MSA saw FIA as too liberal and too focused on socialization and cultural identity rather than on the need for Islamic work in America. MSA's leaders considered educating Muslim Americans about Islam an important first step. The next step in their view was to translate this educational mission into an Islamic identity rather than a cultural one. In addition, MSA sought to build upon the revival of Islam in the aftermath of the Iranian Revolution. In their view, these religious values needed to inform Muslim-American political advocacy. These leaders were opposed to a compromise that would allow the inclusion of more secular Muslim Americans as they made the transition from students to community.

During this same period, global Islamic organizations funded by Saudi petrodollars and the Muslim World League sought to engage with organizations like the Muslim Students Association of the US & Canada (MSA) (GhaneaBassiri 2012, 310). This engagement signified heightened activity among Islamic organizations globally as well as in the United States.

The Islamic Society of North America (ISNA) and the Muslim Community Association of the US & Canada (MCA) were incorporated in the state of Indiana as nonprofit organizations on July 14, 1981, as the result of a consensus among the Council of Presidents (*Islamic Horizons* 1981b, 1).[7] ISNA inherited MSA's assets and much of its operating structure, staff, and accomplished work. ISNA also continued MSA's community and national activities. The executive council consisted of a president and two vice presidents (US and Canada) elected by the membership of ISNA, the past president of ISNA, and five members appointed by the ISNA president with the approval of the Majlis Ash-Shura (*Islamic Horizons* 1981a, 8).

ISNA's comprehensive board sought to balance the needs of the general membership and the constituent and affiliated organizations that would embrace ISNA as their umbrella organization. The Majlis Ash-Shura was required to meet twice a year and was responsible for establishing the organization's policies. The executive council was made responsible for the oversight of the secretary general and the secretary general for the day-to-day management of operations and ultimately for implementing the organization's mission.

The Secretariat of ISNA was located in Plainfield, Indiana. The 134-acre campus, built at a cost of more than $3.4 million, was situated near the Indianapolis International Airport where it remains to this day.[8] All asserts of the MSA and ISNA were required to be invested by NAIT and all properties to be held in trust with NAIT. ISNA's community engagement by facilitating the establishment of Islamic centers and schools brought important institutions into the NAIT family. Many Islamic centers that were established after 1980 often included in their bylaws that their assets would be placed in trust in NAIT, they would affiliate with ISNA, and all disputes would be arbitrated or mediated by ISNA. Therefore, NAIT helped local communities by ensuring that their assets were invested prudently through a pooled fund and their properties were held in trust, while ISNA was responsible for community development.

NAIT was established by the leaders of MSA and ISNA in the hopes of furthering Islamic work in the United States, to strengthen the efforts of MSA (and later ISNA) by establishing a contemporary waqf within the US legal context. As they state:

> The young Muslim Student's Association of America and Canada helped to launch NAIT in 1973 as a waqf or trust organization. Even though Muslims have been immigrating to the United States since the founding of the nation, many people and communities ultimately lost or abandoned their Islamic heritage due to social, and political, reasons. Indeed, many indigenous masajid and centers were lost or forgotten. To prevent this in the future, the organizers believed that creating a waqf or general trust to safeguard the properties of masajid and Islamic centers would be vital for the growth and maintenance of the American Muslim community. (North American Islamic Trust (NAIT) n.d.)

NAIT's waqf program is a variant of the conventional trust/endowment program, because of two important aspects of waqf: the perpetual status of the waqf properties and the unalterable sanctity of the will of the donor. Even donors cannot alter their intent at a later time. Thus, NAIT is unique among national Muslim nonprofit organizations. However, NAIT does not manage, organize, or interfere with masjids or Islamic centers. Each masjid or Islamic center is independently organized, managed, and controlled. NAIT serves as record owner of the property in the capacity of a trustee for the local community. While the decision-making body of a nonprofit corporation can dispose of or encumber communal property, NAIT management cannot do so to waqf properties.

Islamic Relief USA

Islamic Relief USA is arguably one of the most successful US Muslim nonprofit organizations in terms of funds raised. Since its establishment in 1993, it has raised nearly a billion dollars. In 2021, Islamic Relief USA raised nearly $140 million, the largest amount any US Muslim-led nonprofit organization raised. It survived the government's intense scrutiny of US Muslim international humanitarian organizations after September 11, 2001. In light of this federal scrutiny, Islamic Relief USA took proactive steps to engage with Charity Navigator and earn its coveted "four-star" rating. This attempt to demonstrate transparency, best practices, and efficiency helped to further internal legitimacy with Muslim donors in the United States and also provided external legitimacy with compliance and regulatory agencies. By 2014, Islamic Relief USA was raising over $100 million a year serving over ten million beneficiaries in 42 countries ("Islamic Relief Worldwide Annual Report and Financial Statements" 2014). Of this amount, nearly $40 million came from gifts-in-kind.

In 2014, Islamic Relief USA sought to deepen its engagement with Muslim donors and find additional resources to sustain their programs. They established a separate nonprofit organization called Islamic Relief Waqf (IRW). IRW was an independent nonprofit for several reasons. First, there was a belief that much of the work of this institution would be to manage and invest assets. IR USA sought to have experts in the field of investments to serve on the board of this new organization. This was an area of expertise that IR USA felt it did not have. Second, in a post-9/11 environment, there was a feeling that separating these assets would result in a diversification of risk, where unfair government scrutiny of Muslim nonprofit organizations has become increasingly intrusive.

Islamic Relief USA seeded this nonprofit organization with $5 million for its investments. IRW hired Faisal Khan as its first director. Khan was an expert on investing and managing funds. At this stage, he needed to gain experience in raising funds or running a nonprofit organization. They also hired Erum Siddiqui to serve as program manager. Siddiqui came from the educational nonprofit sector and had some experience in the operation of nonprofits. These first two hires indicated the Islamic Relief USA boards' belief that the main task of IRW was to manage funds and that establishing a waqf—along with the legitimacy that Islamic Relief provided as the largest Muslim nonprofit organization in the United States—would be enough to inspire Muslim-American donors to invest. Perhaps missing from this analysis was the difficult nature of capital campaign fundraising and major gift donors. By 2022, IRW assets had grown by $3 million, largely through investment gains, while still managing to engage with Muslim donors to raise additional funds. Here are some challenges that Islamic Relief is working to resolve today: (1) Muslims in the United States do not have a uniform understanding of what a waqf is. Some believe that it is an endowment that funds social good, while some connect it to specific projects. Others may consider it to be tangible assets like real estate, farms, and operation businesses; (2) how to raise funds for IRW in a way that does not impact the fundraising for Islamic Relief USA. Being independent, yet interconnected, necessitates having a uniform strategy; and (3) IRW was established as an investment organization rather than a fundraising nonprofit organization.

It is important to note that on establishment, the Islamic Relief USA board chose that the new institution be called "Waqf." It suggested an attempt to reengage and reinvigorate an Islamic institution that has long been seen as a symbol of pride within the Islamic imagination. It also suggests that Islamic

Relief USA considered US laws to be broad enough to establish their vision of what a waqf should look like in contemporary society.

American Muslim Community Foundation

The American Muslim Community Foundation (AMCF) was established as a tax-exempt organization in 2016 in California. Inspired by the cash waqf from Islamic tradition and the modern-day community foundation, it is a unique example of the Islamic practice of the waqf system embracing an American philanthropic institution. It was cofounded by Muhi Khwaja who had extensive development experience within the Muslim-American nonprofit sector and more recently in the American Red Cross. Khwaja is originally from Michigan and was part of a very civically engaged community that has resulted in innovative Muslim-American leaders and nonprofit institutions. In 2017, AMCF raised $261,636, which dramatically grew to $732,364 in 2018 and $1,150,452 in 2019. Since its founding, AMCF has distributed over $9 million to more than 400 nonprofits. AMCF introduces itself by featuring a quote by Shaykh Ahmadu Bamba of Senegal in which he shares pathways to paradise: "Everyone who has passed desires to return and carry an additional work for their benefit in the Afterlife. Giving charity is an affirmation in our faith, purifies our wealth, protects us from calamity, expiates our sins, brings joys to who receive it." AMCF manages a number of donor-advised funds through which Muslim-American donors are encouraged to give sustainably and strategically. In 2021, AMCF hired its first full-time executive director, Sarah Alfaham. In 2018, AMCF started capacity-building for nonprofit organizations, including fiscal sponsorship. In 2019, AMCF launched Giving Circles and in 2020 it established a nonprofit accelerator. As one of the first Muslim community foundations, it has an opportunity to pave the way in illustrating the Islamic practice of the cash waqf through a contemporary American philanthropic form that is more than 100 years old. AMCF is still in its infancy. AMCF offers donors and nonprofit institutions the ability to establish endowments that are invested in ways that are permissible in Islam. As of 2022, AMCF does not invest in or focus on real estate as its investment or service delivery strategy.

El-Hibri Foundation

The El-Hibri family established the El-Hibri Foundation in 2001. It is a tribute to the memory of Ibrahim El-Hibri (1936–2007), who made a substantial gift to the foundation to continue his family's long commitment to helping the less fortunate and promoting interfaith understanding. These funds are invested in a building that houses the foundation and investments that yield income for its programs and grant funding. It provides grants to Muslim organizations, allies of Muslim organizations, and orphans in Lebanon.

Ibrahim El-Hibri, a successful businessman and devout Muslim married to a Christian, believed in the commonality of the three monotheistic religions— Christianity, Judaism, and Islam—and stressed their similarities instead of their differences. His focus on tolerance, civic engagement, and social responsibility was expressed in many philanthropic endeavors.

Ibrahim El-Hibri's legacy has been carried on by his siblings, his children, and his grandchildren and their families. Initially, the foundation was an extension of the family philanthropic investments in the Muslim community in the United States, interfaith activities, and supporting orphans in Lebanon. Its signature investment was to purchase a building in the heart of Washington, DC, that serves as a hub for its activities and as a place where many programs that further its strategy to increase interfaith understanding and to uplift Muslim-American communities have been hosted.

The foundation hired Farhan Latif, who developed a cohesive long-term strategy to further the family's philanthropic goals. Latif was the COO of the Institute of Social Policy and Understanding and an important Muslim-American leader. As someone who has been a boundary-spanner, he has been able to implement important philanthropic grant programs, public events, and upskilling of Muslim leaders and nonprofit institutions. Inspired by the founder's devout faith, El-Hibri Foundation is another example of Muslims seeking to further their religious devotion beyond their lifetime by adopting an American philanthropic legal form.

Table 6.1 shows the typology of American waqfs.

Table 6.1   Typology of Muslim-American waqfs

	North American Islamic Trust	El-Hibri Foundation	Islamic Relief USA Waqf	American Muslim Community Foundation
US legal designation	Trust	Family or operating foundation	Endowment	Community foundation
Waqf type	Hybrid waqf (real estate-cash)	Foundation modeled on waqf	Waqf	Cash waqf
Identifies as waqf?	Explicitly stated	Not explicitly stated	Explicitly stated	Not explicitly stated
Religiously inspired?	Yes	Yes	Yes	Yes

	North American Islamic Trust	El-Hibri Foundation	Islamic Relief USA Waqf	American Muslim Community Foundation
Real estate investment	Partial	Partial	Partial	No
Non-real estate investment	Yes	Yes	Yes	Yes
Paid staff	Yes	Yes	Yes	Yes
Funds only Muslims	Yes	No	No	Yes
Claims Shariʿa-compliant investment	Yes	Unknown	Yes	Yes

CONCLUSION

The philanthropic practice of waqf, which has developed and transformed drastically over time, is a powerful example of how religious traditions adapt to the legal, political, and economic circumstances of their environment while also maintaining important discursive continuity with their founding concepts and practices. The intense transformation of the waqf over the last 200 years was a result of adaptation as much as it was the outcome of colonial destruction. When the waqf was implemented during the time of the Prophet Muhammad, it drew upon existing knowledge and local traditions, some of which predated Islam. The idea to preserve current wealth for future social good may not be a uniquely Muslim idea, but Muslims have likely helped shape this idea through their legal form of waqf.

In this chapter, we have sketched a brief history of waqf from its earliest incarnations through its medieval, early modern, and modern transformations. Our goal has been to paint the waqf as a dynamic legal tool for the private provision of social goods in a way that links Islamic philanthropy to socioeconomic development and religious acts of piety.

We have also attempted to pursue a general line of reasoning about the use of the waqf as model and concept in the context of American Muslim organizations. Many sing the praises of the waqf, but few have attempted to establish a waqf in the United States given the different legal structure of religious nonprofit institutions. However, how the waqf has served as a model and guide for US-based Muslim organizations and associations is worth pursuing in more granular detail.

The Muslim groups in the United States that we described here have sought to find a US legal form to help practice their religious tradition of waqf. The legal form these Muslim organizations selected as the best way to achieve their goals (as modeled on the waqf) is different depending upon the founders' purpose. Some have selected the US foundation; some have chosen community foundations, some have chosen charitable trusts or 501(c)(3) forms, while others have chosen nonprofit endowments as the legal form to house their waqf. Similarly, due to increased government surveillance of Muslim organizations, especially those which deal with financial assets, as well as the divergent understandings of waqfs among US Muslims, not all have sought to name their entity a waqf. Some have begun with that name but then changed it to a more generic American term due to the lack of consensus on what a waqf is in the contemporary context. Future research could build on this study's portrayal of how many religious traditions in Muslim-majority contexts have adopted versions of the waqf to similarly endow their institutions and causes.

One of the challenges of the modern Muslim waqf is that in Muslim-majority contexts it is highly regulated and is perceived to be mismanaged by state institutions. Religious debate and confusion about its current scope make the development of the waqf in the modern context difficult to practice. It is due to these unique challenges that our analysis of Muslim Americans is useful for examining how some Muslims seek to practice this Islamic tradition in a contemporary context. As we have shared, Muslims in the United States are highly diverse and provide different applications of the same idea within one geographic context. While they do not represent how Muslims across the world practice, they provide important insights on how different Muslims can practice this tradition in diverse ways. Due to the highly legal nature of the waqf system in Islamic religion and the practical need to preserve wealth overtime, examining how waqfs are practiced within different legal contexts is an important area for future research, both in a Muslim-majority context and a -minority context.

NOTES

1. For an example of waqf creation as a philanthropic activity that simultaneously serves pious as well as political aims (i.e., as acts of citizenship, yet not citizenship in liberal terms), especially in the case of women founders, see Isin and Üstündağ (2008). See also Hoexter (1998, 481).
2. The modern boundaries between public and private spheres are historically contested and should not be taken for granted as natural oppositions, especially in the context of late antique and medieval Muslim societies. See Asad (2003).
3. For a critique of Kuran, see Çizakça (2010). See Crow (2013) for a comparison between Kuran and Çizakça's views, though not without its own issues.
4. North American Islamic Trust Inc., Articles of Incorporation, May 23, 1973.

5.   North American Islamic Trust Inc., Articles of Incorporation, December 29, 2014.
6.   NAIT website.
7.   The Council of Presidents consisted of the leaders of the Muslim Students Association of the US & Canada (MSA), the Islamic Medical Association of North America (IMANA), the Association of Muslim Social Scientists (AMSS), and the Association of Muslim Scientists and Engineers (AMSE).
8.   The project was made possible through a donation from the son of King Faisal of Saudi Arabia to purchase the land and the Emir of Qatar to pay for the construction of the building. The building consisted of a library, offices for staff, a prayer area, and a basement for community activities. The campus consisted of four buildings (that existed at the time of purchase) and a lake to help host camps envisioned by the founders of the ISNA. These buildings were renamed: Ansar House, Huda House, Salam House, and Muhajireen House. Ansar House was the ISNA's headquarters until the main building was completed. Muhajireen House was designated as the guest house for frequent national and international visitors to the ISNA.

Bibliography

Abbasi, Muhammad Zubair. 2012. "The Classical Islamic Law of Waqf: A Concise Introduction." *Arab Law Quarterly* 26 (2): 121–53.

Abbasi, Muhammad Zubair. 2014. "Islamic Law and Social Change: An Insight into the Making of Anglo-Muhammadan Law." *Journal of Islamic Studies* 25 (3): 325–49.

Abdul Aziz, Ahmad Hafiz Bin, Wei Zhang, Baharom Abdul Hamid, Ziyaad Mahomed, Said Bouheraoua, Noor Suhaida Kasri, and Mohamed Al-Amine Sano. 2019. "Maximizing Social Impact Through Waqf Solutions (English)." Washington, DC: World Bank Group. http://documents.worldbank.org/curated/en/930461562218730622/Maximizing-Social-Impact-Through-Waqf-Solutions

Abdullah, Mohammad. 2018. "Waqf, Sustainable Development Goals (SDGs) and Maqasid al-Shariah." *International Journal of Social Economics* 45 (1): 158–72. https://doi.org/10.1108/IJSE-10-2016-0295

Abraham, Danielle Widmann. 2018. "Zakat as Practical Theodicy: Precarity and the Critique of Gender in Muslim India." *Journal of Muslim Philanthropy & Civil Society* 4 (2): 120–48.

Abu-Shamsieh, Kamal. 2020. "The Application of Maqāsid Al-Shariah in Islamic Chaplaincy." In *Islamic Law and Ethics*, edited by David Vishanoff, 76–108. London: International Institute of Islamic Thought.

Adachi, Mari. 2018. "Discourses of Institutionalization of Zakat Management System in Contemporary Indonesia: Effect of the Revitalization of Islamic Economics." *International Journal of Zakat* 3 (1): 25–35. https://doi.org/10.37706/ijaz.v3i1.71

Adam, Thomas. 2020. "From Waqf to Foundation: The Case for a Global and Integrated History of Philanthropy." *Journal of Muslim Philanthropy & Civil Society* 4 (1). https://scholarworks.iu.edu/iupjournals/index.php/muslimphilanthropy/article/view/1916

Ahmed, Habib. 2019. "Legal Constraints to the Development of Waqf." In *Revitalization of Waqf for Socio-Economic Development, Volume II*, edited by Khalifa Mohamed Ali, M. Kabir Hassan, and Abd elrahman Elzahi Saaid Ali, 153–74. Springer International Publishing. https://doi.org/10.1007/978-3-030-18449-0_8

Akhtar, Zia. 2013. "Charitable Trusts and Waqfs: Their Parallels, Registration Process, and Tax Reliefs in the United Kingdom." *Statute Law Review* 34 (3): 281–95. https://doi.org/10.1093/slr/hms045

Al-Ghazali, Abu Hamid. 1966. *Mysteries of Almsgiving*. Translated by Nabih Amin Faris. American University of Beirut Centennial Publications.

Ali, Khalifa Mohamed, M. Kabir Hassan, and Abd elrahman Elzahi Saaid Ali, eds. 2019. *Revitalization of Waqf for Socio-Economic Development*, Vol. 1. Palgrave Macmillan. https://link.springer.com/book/10.1007/978-3-030-18445-2

Alsultany, Evelyn. 2007. "Selling American Diversity and Muslim American Identity through Nonprofit Advertising Post-9/11." *American Quarterly* 59 (3): 593–622.

Alterman, J. B., S. Hunter, and A. L. Phillips. 2005. *The Idea and Practice of Philanthropy in the Muslim World*. US Agency for International Development.

al-Tirmidhi. n.d. "Jami` At-Tirmidhi 1376—The Chapters On Judgements From The Messenger of Allah." Accessed May 27, 2023. https://sunnah.com/tirmidhi:1376

Ammani, Sahiba Abdullahi, Safiyya Abubakar Abba, and Kabiru Isa Dandago. 2014. "Zakah on Employment Income in Muslims Majority States of Nigeria: Any Cause for Alarm?" *Procedia—Social and Behavioral Sciences*, International Conference on Accounting Studies 2014, ICAS 2014, August 18–19, 2014, Kuala Lumpur, Malaysia, 164 (December): 305–14. https://doi.org/10.1016/j.sbspro.2014.11.081

Amr, Hady, Mogahed, Dalia, and Marshall, Katherine. 2008. *Human Development in the Muslim World*. Brooking Institute. https://www.brookings.edu/wp-content/uploads/2016/06/02_islamic_world_amr.pdf

Anastasopoulos, L. Jason, and Andrew B. Whitford. 2019. "Machine Learning for Public Administration Research, With Application to Organizational Reputation." *Journal of Public Administration Research and Theory* 29 (3): 491–510. https://doi.org/10.1093/jopart/muy060

Anderson, J. N. D. 1951. "The Religious Element in Waqf Endowments." *Journal of The Royal Central Asian Society* 38 (4): 292–9.

Anderson, J. N. D. 1952. "Recent Developments in Shari'a Law Ix: The Waqf System." *The Muslim World* 42 (4): 257–76. https://doi.org/10.1111/j.1478-1913.1952.tb02160.x

Anderson, J. N. D. 1959. "Waqfs in East Africa." *Journal of African Law* 3 (3): 152–64.

Anderson, Jon W. 2003. "New Media, New Publics: Reconfiguring the Public Sphere of Islam." *Social Research* 70 (3): 887–906.

Asad, Talal. 1986. "The Idea of an Anthropology of Islam." Center for Contemporary Arab Studies, Georgetown University.

Asad, Talal. 1992. "Conscripts of Western Civilization." In *Dialectical Anthropology: Essays in Honor of Stanley Diamond*, edited by Christine Ward Gailey, 1, Civilization in Crisis: 333–51. University Presses of Florida.

Asad, Talal. 2003. *Formations of the Secular: Christianity, Islam, Modernity*. Stanford University Press.

Aslett, Kevin, Nora Webb Williams, Andreu Casas, Wesley Zuidema, and John Wilkerson. 2020. "What Was the Problem in Parkland? Using Social Media to Measure the Effectiveness of Issue Frames." SSRN Scholarly Paper ID 3383797. Rochester, NY: Social Science Research Network. https://doi.org/10.2139/ssrn.3383797

Atia, Mona. 2013. *Building a House in Heaven: Pious Neoliberalism and Islamic Charity in Egypt*. University of Minnesota Press.

Awaliah Kasri, Rahmatina. 2013. "Giving Behaviors in Indonesia: Motives and Marketing Implications for Islamic Charities." *Journal of Islamic Marketing* 4 (3): 306–24. https://doi.org/10.1108/JIMA-05-2011-0044

Bagby, Ihsan. 2021. "American Mosques and Their Various Approaches in Understanding Islam." *Theology Today* 78 (3) (October 1): 276–84. https://doi.org/10.1177/00405736211030228

Bagby, Ihsan, Paul M. Perl, and Brian T Froehle. 2001. *The Mosque in America: A National Portrait: A Report from the Mosque Study Project*. Washington, DC: Council on American-Islamic Relations.

Bagozzi, Benjamin E., and Daniel Berliner. 2018. "The Politics of Scrutiny in Human Rights Monitoring: Evidence from Structural Topic Models of US State Department Human Rights Reports." *Political Science Research and Methods* 6 (4): 661–77. https://doi.org/10.1017/psrm.2016.44

Bano, Masooda. 2012. *The Rational Believer Choices and Decisions in the Madrasas of Pakistan*. Cornell University Press. http://site.ebrary.com/id/10547368

Barman, Emily. 2017. "The Social Bases of Philanthropy." *Annual Review of Sociology* 43 (1): 271–90. https://doi.org/10.1146/annurev-soc-060116-053524

Barnes, John Robert. 1987. *An Introduction to Religious Foundations in the Ottoman Empire*. Brill.

Bashear, Suliman. 1993. "On the Origins and Development of the Meaning of Zakāt in Early Islam." *Arabica* 40 (1): 84–113.

Bassiouni, M. Cherif, and Gamal M. Badr. 2001. "The Shari'ah: Sources, Interpretation, and Rule-Making." *UCLA Journal of Islamic and Near Eastern Law* 135.

Ba-Yunus, Ilyas, and Kassim Kone. 2006. *Muslims in the United States*. Greenwood Publishing Group.

Bekkers, René, and Theo Schuyt. 2008. "And Who Is Your Neighbor? Explaining Denominational Differences in Charitable Giving and Volunteering in the Netherlands." *Review of Religious Research* 50 (1): 74–96.

Bekkers, René, and Pamala Wiepking. 2011a. "A Literature Review of Empirical Studies of Philanthropy: Eight Mechanisms That Drive Charitable Giving." *Nonprofit and Voluntary Sector Quarterly* 40 (5): 924–73. https://doi.org/10.1177/0899764010380927

Bekkers, René, and Pamala Wiepking. 2011b. "Who Gives? A Literature Review of Predictors of Charitable Giving Part One: Religion, Education, Age and Socialisation." *Voluntary Sector Review* 2 (3): 337–65. https://doi.org/10.1332/204080511X6087712

Believers Bail Out. n.d.a "About Us." Accessed May 27, 2023. https://believersbailout.org/about/

Believers Bail Out. n.d.b "Believers Bail Out." Accessed May 27, 2023. https://believersbailout.org/

Benthall, Jonathan. 1999. "Financial Worship: The Quranic Injunction to Almsgiving." *The Journal of the Royal Anthropological Institute* 5 (1): 27–42. https://doi.org/10.2307/2660961

Benthall, Jonathan. 2017. "Charity." Edited by Felix Stein. *Cambridge Encyclopedia of Anthropology*, December. https://doi.org/10.29164/17charity

Berman, Edward H. 1983. *The Influence of the Carnegie, Ford, and Rockefeller Foundations on American Foreign Policy: The Ideology of Philanthropy*. SUNY Press.

Berman, Eli. 2009. *Radical, Religious, and Violent: The New Economics of Terrorism*. The MIT Press.

Bhati, A., and D. McDonnell. 2020. "Success in an Online Giving Day: The Role of Social Media in Fundraising." https://doi.org/10.1177/0899764019868849

Billis, David. 2020. "Hybrid Organisations in the Overlapping Territory with the Personal World." In *Handbook on Hybrid Organisations*. Edward Elgar Publishing.

Bird, Frederick B. 1982. "A Comparative Study of The Work of Charity in Christianity and Judaism." *The Journal of Religious Ethics* 10 (1): 144–69.

Bobkowski, Piotr S., and Lisa D. Pearce. 2011. "Baring Their Souls in Online Profiles or Not? Religious Self-Disclosure in Social Media." *Journal for the Scientific Study of Religion* 50 (4): 744–62. https://doi.org/10.1111/j.1468-5906.2011.01597.x

Bourdieu, Pierre. 1991. "Genesis and Structure of the Religious Field." *Comparative Social Research* 13: 1–44.

Bremner, Robert H. 1988. *American Philanthropy*. University of Chicago Press.

Brinkerhoff, Jennifer M. 2014. "Diaspora Philanthropy: Lessons from a Demographic Analysis of the Coptic Diaspora." *Nonprofit and Voluntary Sector Quarterly* 43 (6): 969–92. https://doi.org/10.1177/0899764013488835

Brubaker, Pamela Jo, and Michel M. Haigh. 2017. "The Religious Facebook Experience: Uses and Gratifications of Faith-Based Content." *Social Media + Society* 3 (2): 2056305117703723. https://doi.org/10.1177/2056305117703723

Bukhari, Muhammad al-. n.d.a "Al-Adab Al-Mufrad 225—Good Conduct." Sunnah. Com. Accessed May 26, 2023. https://sunnah.com/adab:225

Bukhari, Muhammad al-. n.d.b "Sahih Al-Bukhari 6021—Good Manners and Form (Al-Adab)." Sunnah.Com. Accessed April 11, 2023. https:// sunnah .com/ bukhari: 6021

Bulut, Mehmet, and Cem Korkut. 2019. "Ottoman Cash Waqfs: An Alternative Financial System." *Insight Turkey* 21 (3): 91–112.

Butcher, Jacqueline, and Christopher J. Einolf, eds. 2018. *Perspectives on Volunteering: Voices from the South*. Softcover reprint of the original 1st ed. 2017 edition. Springer.

CAF World Giving Index. 2019. 10. London, UK: Charities Aid Foundation. https:// www .cafonline .org/ docs/ default -source/ about -us -publications/ caf _wgi _10th _edition_ report_2712a_web_101019.pdf

Campbell, David A., Kristina T. Lambright, and Christopher J. Wells. 2014. "Looking for Friends, Fans, and Followers? Social Media Use in Public and Nonprofit Human Services." *Public Administration Review* 74 (5): 655–63. https://doi.org/10.1111/ puar.12261

Campbell, Heidi A. 2012. *Digital Religion: Understanding Religious Practice in New Media Worlds*. Routledge.

Castillo, Marco, Ragan Petrie, and Clarence Wardell. 2014. "Fundraising through Online Social Networks: A Field Experiment on Peer-to-Peer Solicitation." *Journal of Public Economics* 114 (June): 29–35. https://doi.org/10.1016/j.jpubeco.2014.01 .002

Chamberlain, Judi. 1990. "The Ex-Patient's Movement: Where We've Been and Where We're Going." *Journal of Mind and Behavior* 11 (3–4): 323–36.

Cheong, Pauline Hope. 2012. *Digital Religion, Social Media, and Culture: Perspectives, Practices, and Futures*. Digital Formations, Vol. 78. P. Lang.

Chuang, Jason, John D. Wilkerson, Rebecca Weiss, Dustin Tingley, Brandon M. Stewart, Margaret E. Roberts, Forough Poursabzi-Sangdeh, Justin Grimmer, Leah Findlater, and Jordan Boyd-Graber. 2014. "Computer-Assisted Content Analysis: Topic Models for Exploring Multiple Subjective Interpretations." In *Advances in Neural Information Processing Systems Workshop on Human-Propelled Machine Learning*, 1–9.

Çizakça, Murat. 2000. *A History of Philanthropic Foundations: The Islamic World from the Seventh Century to the Present*. Boğaziçi University Press.

Cizakca, Murat. 2010. "Was Shari'ah Indeed the Culprit?" MPRA Paper. https://ideas .repec.org//p/pra/mprapa/22865.html

Çizakça, Murat. 2011. Review of *Review of The Long Divergence: How Islamic Law Held Back the Middle East*, by Timur Kuran. *Review of Middle East Studies* 45 (1): 117–19.

Crow, Karim Douglas. 2013. "Islam, Capitalism and Underdevelopment: Timur Kuran and Murat Cizakca on the Great Divergence." *ICR Journal* 4 (3): 371–90.

Curtis, Daniel W., Van Evans, and Ram A. Cnaan. 2015. "Charitable Practices of Latter-Day Saints." *Nonprofit and Voluntary Sector Quarterly* 44 (1): 146–62. https://doi.org/10.1177/0899764013508010

Curtis IV, Edward. 2009. *Muslims in America: A Short History*. Oxford University Press.

Dallal, Ahmad. 2004. "The Islamic Institution of Waqf: A Historical Overview." In *Islam and Social Policy*, edited by Stephen P. Heyneman, 13–43. Vanderbilt University Press.

Daly, Marwa El. 2012. *Challenges and Potentials of Channeling Local Philanthropy Towards Development and Social Justice and the Role of Waqf (Islamic and Arab-Civic Endowments) in Building Community Foundations: The Case of Egypt.* Humboldt Universität zu Berlin, Philosophische Fakultät III.

Dekker, Paul, and Loek Halman. 2005. *The Value of Volunteering. Cross-Cultural Perspectives*. Springer.

Diouf, Sylviane. 1999. "'Ṣadaqa' Among African Muslims Enslaved in the Americas." *Journal of Islamic Studies* 10 (1): 22–32.

Diouf, Sylviane. 2013. *Servants of Allah: African Muslims Enslaved in the Americas, 15th Anniversary Edition*. NYU Press.

Diouf, Sylviane. 2022. "Enslaved Philanthropists: Charity, Community, and Freedom in the Americas." *Journal of Muslim Philanthropy & Civil Society* 6 (1). https://scholarworks.iu.edu/iupjournals/index.php/muslimphilanthropy/article/view/5338

Duderija, A. 2014. *Maqasid Al-Shari'a and Contemporary Reformist Muslim Thought: An Examination*. Springer.

Eck, Diana L. 2013. "The Religious Gift: Hindu, Buddhist, and Jain Perspectives on Dana." *Social Research* 80 (2): 359–79.

Eckel, Catherine C., and Philip J. Grossman. 2004. "Giving to Secular Causes by the Religious and Nonreligious: An Experimental Test of the Responsiveness of Giving to Subsidies." *Nonprofit and Voluntary Sector Quarterly* 33 (2): 271–89. https://doi.org/10.1177/0899764004263423

Eikenberry, Angela M., and Jodie Drapal Kluver. 2004. "The Marketization of the Nonprofit Sector: Civil Society at Risk?" *Public Administration Review* 64 (2): 132–40. https://doi.org/10.1111/j.1540–6210.2004.00355.x

Eimhjellen, Ivar Sognnæs. 2014. "Internet Communication: Does It Strengthen Local Voluntary Organizations?" *Nonprofit and Voluntary Sector Quarterly* 43 (5): 890–909. https://doi.org/10.1177/0899764013487996

Einolf, Christopher J. 2017. "Cross-National Differences in Charitable Giving in the West and the World." *VOLUNTAS: International Journal of Voluntary and Nonprofit Organizations* 28 (2): 472–91. https://doi.org/10.1007/s11266-016-9758-4

El Haj, Hatem El. 2021. "Zakat Eligibility of Islamic Organizations." *MuslimMatters.Org* (blog). July 20, 2021. https://muslimmatters.org/2021/07/20/zakat-eligibility-of-islamic-organizations/

Everatt, David, Adam Habib, Brij Maharaj, and Annsilla Nyar. 2005. "Patterns of Giving in South Africa." *Voluntas* 16 (3): 275–91. https://doi.org/10.1007/s11266-005-7725-z

Everett, Jim A. C., Omar Sultan Haque, and David G. Rand. 2016. "How Good Is the Samaritan, and Why? An Experimental Investigation of the Extent and Nature of Religious Prosociality Using Economic Games." *Social Psychological and Personality Science* 7 (3): 248–55. https://doi.org/10.1177/1948550616632577

Everton, Sean. 2019. "Networks and Religion: Ties That Bind, Loose, Build Up, and Tear Down." *Journal of Social Structure* 16 (1). https://doi.org/10.21307/joss-2019-020

Fahrenthold, Stacy. 2014. "Sound Minds in Sound Bodies: Transnational Philanthropy and Patriotic Masculinity in Al-Nadi Al-Homsi and Syrian Brazil, 1920–32." *International Journal of Middle East Studies* 46 (2): 259–83.

Fahrenthold, Stacy. 2019. *Between the Ottomans and the Entente: The First World War in the Syrian and Lebanese Diaspora, 1908–1925.* Oxford University Press.

Falk, Armin, Anke Becker, Thomas Dohmen, Benjamin Enke, David Huffman, and Uwe Sunde. 2018. "Global Evidence on Economic Preferences." *The Quarterly Journal of Economics* 133 (4): 1645–92. https://doi.org/10.1093/qje/qjy013

Falus, Orsolya. 2020. "Piae Causae Foundations, Waqfs, Trusts. Legal-Historical Interactions." *POLGÁRI SZEMLE: GAZDASÁGI ÉS TÁRSADALMI FOLYÓIRAT* 16 (4–6): 353–60.

Farrow, Harmonie, and Y. Connie Yuan. 2011. "Building Stronger Ties With Alumni Through Facebook to Increase Volunteerism and Charitable Giving." *Journal of Computer-Mediated Communication* 16 (3): 445–64. https://doi.org/10.1111/j.1083 -6101.2011.01550.x

Fateh Ahmad, Husnain, and Hadia Majid. 2021a. "Disaggregating the Effects of Inequality on Informal Giving: Evidence From Pakistan." *Nonprofit and Voluntary Sector Quarterly*, May, 08997640211013899. https:// doi .org/ 10 .1177/ 0899 7640211013899

Fateh Ahmad, Husnain, and Hadia Majid. 2021b. "Disaggregating the Effects of Inequality on Informal Giving: Evidence From Pakistan." *Nonprofit and Voluntary Sector Quarterly*, May. https://doi.org/10.1177/0899 7640211013899

Fauzia, Amelia. 2008. "Faith and the State: A History of Islamic Philanthropy in Indonesia." http://minerva-access.unimelb.edu.au/handle/11343/35228

Fauzia, Amelia. 2013. *Faith and the State: A History of Islamic Philanthropy in Indonesia.* Brill.

Fisher, Donald. 1983. "The Role of Philanthropic Foundations in the Reproduction and Production of Hegemony: Rockefeller Foundations and the Social Sciences." *Sociology* 17 (2): 206–33.

Forbes, Kevin F., and Ernest M. Zampelli. 2014. "Volunteerism: The Influences of Social, Religious, and Human Capital." *Nonprofit and Voluntary Sector Quarterly* 43 (2): 227–53. https://doi.org/10.1177/0899764012458542

Foucault, Michel. 1995. *Discipline & Punish: The Birth of the Prison.* Translated by Alan Sheridan. Vintage Books.

Fowler, Alan, and Jacob Mwathi Mati. 2019. "African Gifting: Pluralising the Concept of Philanthropy." *VOLUNTAS: International Journal of Voluntary and Nonprofit Organizations* 30 (4): 724–37. https://doi.org/10.1007/s11266-018-00079-z

Freeman, Tyrone McKinley. 2020. *Madam C. J. Walker's Gospel of Giving: Black Women's Philanthropy during Jim Crow.* University of Illinois Press.

Fyall, Rachel, M. Kathleen Moore, and Mary Kay Gugerty. 2018. "Beyond NTEE Codes: Opportunities to Understand Nonprofit Activity Through Mission Statement Content Coding." *Nonprofit and Voluntary Sector Quarterly* 47 (4): 677–701. https://doi.org/10.1177/0899764018768019

García-Colín, Jacqueline Butcher, and Santiago Sordo Ruz. 2016. "Giving Mexico: Giving by Individuals." *Voluntas: International Journal of Voluntary and Nonprofit Organizations* 27 (1): 322–47.

Garcia-Rudolph, Alejandro, Sara Laxe, Joan Saurí, and Montserrat Bernabeu Guitart. 2019. "Stroke Survivors on Twitter: Sentiment and Topic Analysis From a Gender Perspective." *Journal of Medical Internet Research* 21 (8): e14077. https://doi.org/ 10.2196/14077

Gaudiosi, Monica. 1988. "Influence of the Islamic Law of WAQF on the Development of the Trust In England: The Case of Merton College." *University of Pennsylvania Law Review* 136 (4): 1231.

GhaneaBassiri, Kambiz. 2010. *A History of Islam in America: From the New World to the New World Order.* 1st edition. Cambridge University Press.

GhaneaBassiri, Kambiz. 2012. *A History of Islam in America.* Oxford University Press.

Ghazaleh, Pascale, ed. 2011. *Held in Trust: Waqf in the Islamic World.* American University in Cairo Press. http://dx.doi.org/10.5743/cairo/9789774163937.001.0001

Gil, Moshe. 1998. "The Earliest Waqf Foundations." *Journal of Near Eastern Studies* 57 (2): 125–40.

Gill, Anthony J., and Steven J. Pfaff. 2010. "Acting in Good Faith: An Economic Approach to Religious Organizations as Advocacy Groups." In *Advocacy Organizations and Collective Action*, edited by Aseem Prakash and Mary Kay Gugerty, 58–90. Cambridge University Press. https://doi.org/10.1017/CBO9780511762635.005

Ginio, Eyal. 1997. "Violations of Founders' Stipulations in the Sharīʿa Court of Jaffa during the British Mandate." *Islamic Law and Society* 4 (3): 389–415.

Godfrey, John, Elizabeth Branigan, and Sabith Khan. 2017. "Old and New Forms of Giving: Understanding Corporate Philanthropy in India. (Report)." *Voluntas: International Journal of Voluntary and Nonprofit Organizations* 28 (2): 672–96. https://doi.org/10.1007/s11266-016-9693-4

Gomez, Michael A. 2005. *Black Crescent: The Experience and Legacy of African Muslims in the Americas.* Cambridge University Press.

Grimmer, Justin, and Gary King. 2011. "General Purpose Computer-Assisted Clustering and Conceptualization." *Proceedings of the National Academy of Sciences* 108 (7): 2643–50. https://doi.org/10.1073/pnas.1018067108

Grzymała-Busse, Anna. 2023. *Sacred Foundations: The Religious and Medieval Roots of the European State.* Princeton University Press.

Guo, Chao. 2007. "When Government Becomes the Principal Philanthropist: The Effects of Public Funding on Patterns of Nonprofit Governance." *Public Administration Review* 67 (3): 458–73. https://doi.org/10.1111/j.1540-6210.2007.00729.x

Guo, Chao, and Gregory D. Saxton. 2014. "Tweeting Social Change: How Social Media Are Changing Nonprofit Advocacy." *Nonprofit and Voluntary Sector Quarterly* 43 (1): 57–79. https://doi.org/10.1177/089976401247158

Guo, Chao, and Gregory D. Saxton. 2020. *The Quest for Attention: Nonprofit Advocacy in a Social Media Age.* 1st edition. Stanford Business Books.

Hall, Peter Dobkin. 1999. "The Work of Many Hands: A Response to Stanley N. Katz on the Origins of the 'Serious Study' of Philanthropy." *Nonprofit and Voluntary Sector Quarterly* 28 (4): 522–34.

Hall, Peter Dobkin. 2006. "A Historical Overview of Philanthropy, Voluntary Associations, and Nonprofit Organizations in the United States, 1600–2000." *The Nonprofit Sector: A Research Handbook* 2: 32–65.

Hallaq, Wael B. 1989. "Non-Analogical Arguments in Sunni Juridical Qiyās." *Arabica* 36 (3): 286–306.

Hallaq, Wael B. 1990. "Logic, Formal Arguments and Formalization of Arguments in Sunnī Jurisprudence." *Arabica* 37 (3): 315–58.

Hallaq, Wael B. 1997. *A History of Islamic Legal Theories: An Introduction to Sunni Usul al-Fiqh.* Cambridge University Press.

Hallaq, Wael B. 2005. *The Origins and Evolution of Islamic Law.* Cambridge University Press.

Hammer, Juliane, and Omid Safi, eds. 2013. *The Cambridge Companion to American Islam*. Cambridge Companions to Religion. Cambridge University Press. https://doi .org/10.1017/CCO9781139026161

Hanif, Sohail. 2022. "When Worship Meets Taxation: Socio-Political Reflections on the Rules of Zakat." *Islamic Law Blog* (blog). March 31, 2022. https://islamiclaw .blog/2022/03/31/when-worship-meets-taxation-socio-political-reflections-on-the -rules-of-zakat/

Hasan, Samiul. 2015. *Human Security and Philanthropy: Islamic Perspectives and Muslim Majority Country Practices*. Springer.

Hassan, M. Kabir, Mohd Fazlul Karim, and M. Sydul Karim. 2019. "Experiences and Lessons of Cash Waqf in Bangladesh and Other Countries." In *Revitalization of Waqf for Socio-Economic Development, Volume I*, edited by Khalifa Mohamed Ali, M. Kabir Hassan, and Abd elrahman Elzahi Saaid Ali, 59–83. Springer International Publishing. https://doi.org/10.1007/978-3-030-18445-2_5

Heist, H. Daniel, Marquisha Lawrence Scott, Ram A. Cnaan, M. S. Moodithaya, and Matthew R. Bennett. 2021. "The Philanthropic Poor: Prosocial Behavior in Rural India." *Nonprofit and Voluntary Sector Quarterly*, December. https://doi.org/10 .1177/08997640211060087

Henig, David. 2019. "Economic Theologies of Abundance: Halal Exchange and the Limits of Neoliberal Effects in Post-War Bosnia–Herzegovina." *Ethnos* 84 (2): 223–40. https://doi.org/10.1080/00141844.2017.1396233

Hennigan, Peter C. 2004. *The Birth of a Legal Institution: The Formation of the Waqf in Third-Century AH Ḥanafī Legal Discourse*. Brill.

Herrold, Catherine E. 2018. "A Conceptual Model of Foundations' Leadership Capacity in Times of Change: Lessons From Egypt." *Nonprofit and Voluntary Sector Quarterly* 47 (2): 286–303. https://doi.org/10.1177/0899764017746020

Herzog, Patricia Snell, David P. King, Rafia A. Khader, Amy Strohmeier, and Andrew L. Williams. 2020. "Studying Religiosity and Spirituality: A Review of Macro, Micro, and Meso-Level Approaches." *Religions* 11 (9): 437. https://doi.org/10.3390/ rel11090437

Hjarvard, Stig. 2011. "The Mediatisation of Religion: Theorising Religion, Media and Social Change." *Culture and Religion* 12 (2): 119–35. https://doi.org/10.1080/ 14755610.2011.579719

Hoexter, Miriam. 1998. "Waqf Studies in the Twentieth Century: The State of the Art." *Journal of the Economic and Social History of the Orient* 41 (4): 474–95.

Hoexter, Miriam. 2002. "The Waqf and the Public Sphere." In *The Public Sphere in Muslim Societies*, edited by Miriam Hoexter, Shmuel N. Eisenstadt, and Nehemia Levtzion, 119–38. State University of New York Press.

Hofri-Winogradow, Adam S. 2012. "Zionist Settlers and the English Private Trust in Mandate Palestine." *Law and History Review* 30 (3): 813–64.

Hoge, R., and Fenggang Yang. 1994. "Determinants of Religious Giving in American Denominations: Data from Two Nationwide Surveys." *Review of Religious Research* 36 (2): 123–48. https://doi.org/10.2307/3511404

"How Is Zakat Al-Fitrah Calculated?" 2022. IMAM-US.Org. April 12, 2022. https:// imam-us.org/how-is-zakat-al-fitrah-calculated

Howell, Sally. 2010. "Federation of Islamic Associations of the United States and Canada." In *The Encyclopedia of Muslim American History*, edited by Edward Curtis IV, 193. New York: Facts on File, Inc.

Howell, Sally. 2013. "Laying the Groundwork for American Muslim Histories: 1865–1965." In *The Cambridge Companion to American Islam*, edited by Juliane

Hammer and Omid Safi, 45–64. Cambridge Companions to Religion. Cambridge University Press. https://doi.org/10.1017/CCO9781139026161.006

Hussain, Muzammil M., and Philip N. Howard. 2013. "What Best Explains Successful Protest Cascades? ICTs and the Fuzzy Causes of the Arab Spring." *International Studies Review* 15 (1): 48–66. https://doi.org/10.1111/misr.12020

Hustinx, Lesley, Johan von Essen, Jacques Haers, and Sara Mels. 2014. *Religion and Volunteering: Complex, Contested and Ambiguous Relationships*. Springer.

Ibrahim, Abu Ayub Md., and Shahadat Hossain Khan. 2019. "Waqf Management in the Light of Maqasid al Shariah: Bangladesh Perspective." In *Revitalization of Waqf for Socio-Economic Development, Volume II*, edited by Khalifa Mohamed Ali, M. Kabir Hassan, and Abd elrahman Elzahi Saaid Ali, 229–48. Springer International Publishing. https://doi.org/10.1007/978-3-030-18449-0_12

Imam al-Nawawi. n.d. "Riyad As-Salihin 126—The Book of Miscellany." Sunnah. com. Accessed April 11, 2023. https://sunnah.com/riyadussalihin:126

Iqbal, Basit Kareem, and Milad Odabaei. 2021. "Talal Asad: Critical Theory for Political Theology." *Political Theology Network* (blog). May 11, 2021. https://politicaltheology.com/talal-asad/

Isin, Engin F. 2011. "Ottoman Waqfs as Acts of Citizenship." In *Held in Trust: Waqf in the Islamic World*, edited by Pascale Ghazaleh, 209–29. American University in Cairo Press.

Isin, Engin F., and Alexandre Lefebvre. 2005. "The Gift of Law: Greek Euergetism and Ottoman Waqf." *European Journal of Social Theory* 8 (1): 5–23.

Isin, Engin F., and Ebru Üstündağ. 2008. "Wills, Deeds, Acts: Women's Civic Gift-Giving in Ottoman Istanbul." *Gender, Place & Culture* 15 (5): 519–32. https://doi.org/10.1080/09663690802300860

Islamic Horizons. 1981a. "ISNA to Represent Muslims," May 1981.

Islamic Horizons. 1981b. "New Organization Structure Takes Shape—ISNA and MCA Incorporated," August 1981.

"Islamic Relief Worldwide Annual Report and Financial Statements." 2014. Birmingham, UK: Islamic Relief Worldwide.

Jadoon, Zafar, and Samiul Hasan. 2006. "Philanthropy and Third Sector in Pakistan: Overview, Extent, Activities, and Impacts." SSRN Scholarly Paper ID 3009583. Rochester, NY: Social Science Research Network. https://doi.org/10.2139/ssrn.3009583

Johnson, Joan Marie. 2017. *Funding Feminism: Monied Women, Philanthropy, and the Women's Movement, 1870–1967*. University of North Carolina Press.

Jon Alterman, Shireen Hunter, and Ann Phillips. 2005. "The Idea of Philanthropy in the Muslim World." PPC Issue Paper. 5. USAID. https:// csis -website -prod .s3 .amazonaws .com/ s3fs -public/ legacy _files/ files/ media/ csis/ pubs/ the _idea _of _philanthropy_in_the_muslim_world.pdf

Joseph, Sabrina. 2014. "Waqf in Historical Perspective: Online Fatāwā and Contemporary Discourses by Muslim Scholars." *Journal of Muslim Minority Affairs* 34 (4): 425–37.

Jung, Kyujin, and Jesus N. Valero. 2016. "Assessing the Evolutionary Structure of Homeless Network: Social Media Use, Keywords, and Influential Stakeholders." *Technological Forecasting and Social Change* 110 (September 1): 51–60. https://doi.org/10.1016/j.techfore.2015.07.015

Jung, Tobias, Jenny Harrow, and Diana Leat. 2018. "Mapping Philanthropic Foundations' Characteristics: Towards an International Integrative Framework of

Foundation Types." *Nonprofit and Voluntary Sector Quarterly* 47 (5): 893–917. https://doi.org/10.1177/0899764018772135

Kailani, Najib, and Martin Slama. 2020. "Accelerating Islamic Charities in Indonesia: Zakat, Sedekah and the Immediacy of Social Media." *South East Asia Research* 28 (1): 70–86. https://doi.org/10.1080/0967828X.2019.1691939

Kaleem, Ahmad, and Saima Ahmed. 2010. "The Quran and Poverty Alleviation: A Theoretical Model for Charity-Based Islamic Microfinance Institutions (MFIs)." *Nonprofit and Voluntary Sector Quarterly* 39 (3): 409–28. https://doi.org/10.1177/0899764009332466

Karl, Barry D., and Stanley N. Katz. 1987. "Foundations and Ruling Class Elites." *Daedalus* 116 (1): 1–40.

Kasri, Rahmatina A., and Niken Iwani Surya Putri. 2018. "Fundraising Strategies to Optimize Zakat Potential in Indonesia: An Exploratory Qualitative Study." *Al-Iqtishad Journal of Islamic Economics* 1 (10): 1–24. https://doi.org/10.15408/aiq.v10i1.6191

Kassam, Meenaz. 2016. *Philanthropy in India: Promise to Practice*. SAGE Publications India Pvt Ltd.

Kgatle, Mookgo S. 2018. "Social Media and Religion: Missiological Perspective on the Link between Facebook and the Emergence of Prophetic Churches in Southern Africa." *Verbum et Ecclesia* 39 (1): 1–6. https://doi.org/10.4102/ve.v39i1.1848

Khan, Sabith. 2015. "Re-Examining the Policies in the Humanitarian Aid Sector—A Call for Greater 'Value Rationality.'" *Nonprofit Policy Forum* 7 (1): 15–21. https://doi.org/10.1515/npf-2015-0031

Khan, Sabith, and Shariq Siddiqui. 2017. *Islamic Education in the United States and the Evolution of Muslim Nonprofit Institutions*. Edward Elgar Publishing.

Khan, Zara. 2021. "Morally Reimagining the Waqf : Using a Classical Islamic Institution to Dismantle Structural Injustice." *Journal of Muslim Philanthropy & Civil Society* 5 (1). https://scholarworks.iu.edu/iupjournals/index.php/muslimphilanthropy/article/view/3624

King, David P. 2018. "Religion, Charity, and Philanthropy in America." Oxford University Press. https://doi.org/10.1093/acrefore/9780199340378.013.435

Klopp, Richard Lee. 2015. "The Rhetoric of Philanthropy: Scientific Charity as Moral Language." Dissertation, Lilly Family School of Philanthropy, Indiana University. https://doi.org/10.7912/C2/609

Kuran, Timur. 1997. "Islam and Underdevelopment: An Old Puzzle Revisited." Princeton University Press.

Kuran, Timur. 2001. "The Provision of Public Goods under Islamic Law: Origins, Impact, and Limitations of the Waqf System." *Law and Society Review*, 841–98.

Kuran, Timur. 2003. "Islamic Redistribution through Zakat: Historical Record and Modern Realities." In *Poverty and Charity in Middle Eastern Contexts*, edited by Michael Bonner, 275–93. State University of New York Press.

Kuran, Timur. 2016. "Legal Roots of Authoritarian Rule in the Middle East: Civic Legacies of the Islamic Waqf." *The American Journal of Comparative Law* 64 (2): 419–54.

Lacetera, Nicola, Mario Macis, and Angelo Mele. 2016. "Viral Altruism? Charitable Giving and Social Contagion in Online Networks." *Sociological Science* 3 (April): 202–38. https://doi.org/10.15195/v3.a11

Lai, Chih-Hui, Bing She, and Chen-Chao Tao. 2017. "Connecting the Dots: A Longitudinal Observation of Relief Organizations' Representational Networks on

Social Media." *Computers in Human Behavior* 74 (September 1): 224–34. https://doi .org/10.1016/j.chb.2017.04.037

Lajevardi, Nazita. 2019. "The News Media and Portrayals of Muslims Foreign and Domestic." *Maydan* (blog). May 9, 2019. https://themaydan.com/2019/05/the-news -media-and-portrayals-of-muslims-foreign-and-domestic/

Latief, Hilman. 2014. "Contesting Almsgiving in Post-New Order Indonesia." *American Journal of Islam and Society* 31 (1): 16–50. https://doi.org/10.35632/ajis.v31i1.292

Lecy, Jesse, and Jeremy Thornton. 2015. "What Big Data Can Tell Us About Government Awards to the Nonprofit Sector: Using the FAADS." *Nonprofit and Voluntary Sector Quarterly*, December. https://doi.org/10.1177/0899764015620902

Lev, Yaacov. 2005. *Charity, Endowments, and Charitable Institutions in Medieval Islam*. University Press of Florida.

Lewis, David J. 1997. "NGOs, Donors, and the State in Bangladesh." *Annals of the American Academy of Political and Social Science* 554 (November): 33–45.

Lipka, Michael. 2017. "Muslims and Islam: Key Findings in the U.S. and around the World." *Pew Research Center* (blog). 2017. https://www.pewresearch.org/fact-tank/ 2017/08/09/muslims-and-islam-key-findings-in-the-u-s-and-around-the-world/

Litofcenko, Julia, Dominik Karner, and Florentine Maier. 2020. "Methods for Classifying Nonprofit Organizations According to Their Field of Activity: A Report on Semi-Automated Methods Based on Text." *VOLUNTAS: International Journal of Voluntary and Nonprofit Organizations* 31 (1): 227–37. https://doi.org/10.1007/ s11266-019-00181-w

Loewenberg, Frank M. 1994. "On the Development of Philanthropic Institutions in Ancient Judaism: Provisions for Poor Travelers." *Nonprofit and Voluntary Sector Quarterly* 23 (3): 193–207. https://doi.org/10.1177/089976409402300302

Loewenberg, Frank M. 1995. "Financing Philanthropic Institutions in Biblical and Talmudic Times." *Nonprofit and Voluntary Sector Quarterly* 24 (4): 307–20. https:// doi.org/10.1177/089976409502400404

Lovejoy, Kristen, and Gregory D. Saxton. 2012. "Information, Community, and Action: How Nonprofit Organizations Use Social Media." *Journal of Computer-Mediated Communication* 17 (3): 337–53. https://doi.org/10.1111/j.1083–6101.2012.01576.x

Ma, Ji, and Sara Konrath. 2018. "A Century of Nonprofit Studies: Scaling the Knowledge of the Field." https://doi.org/10.1007/s11266-018-00057-5

Ma, Ji, Elise Jing, and Jun Han. 2018. "Predicting Mission Alignment and Preventing Mission Drift: Do Revenue Sources Matter?" *Chinese Public Administration Review* 9 (1): 25–33. https://doi.org/10.22140/cpar.v9i1.173

Macnaghten, Sir William Hay. 1897. *Principles and Precedents of Moohummudan Law, Being a Compliation of Primary Rules Relative to Inheritance, Contracts and Miscellaneous Subjects ...* Madras: Higginbotham and Co.

Mahajneh, Marwan Abu-Ghazaleh, Itay Greenspan, and Muhammad M. Haj-Yahia. 2021. "Zakat Giving to Non-Muslims: Muftis' Attitudes in Arab and Non-Arab Countries." *Journal of Muslim Philanthropy & Civil Society* 5 (2). https:// scholarworks.iu.edu/iupjournals/index.php/muslimphilanthropy/article/view/4889

Makdisi, George. 1981. *The Rise of Colleges: Institutions of Learning in Islam and the West*. Edinburgh University Press.

Malley, Brian. 2004. *How the Bible Works: An Anthropological Study of Evangelical Biblicism*. Rowman Altamira.

Mandaville, Jon E. 1979. "Usurious Piety: The Cash Waqf Controversy in the Ottoman Empire." *International Journal of Middle East Studies* 10 (3): 289–308.

Mattson, Ingrid. 2010. *Zakat in America: The Evolving Role of Charity in Community Cohesion*. The Center on Philanthropy at Indiana University Indiana University-Purdue University Indianapolis.

Maxwell, Sarah P., and Julia L. Carboni. 2016. "Social Media Management." *Nonprofit Management and Leadership* 27 (2): 251–60. https://doi.org/10.1002/nml.21232

McChesney, Robert D. 1991. *Waqf in Central Asia: Four Hundred Years in the History of a Muslim Shrine, 1480–1889*. Vol. 1182. Princeton University Press.

McChesney, Robert D. 1995. *Charity and Philanthropy in Islam: Institutionalizing the Call to Do Good, Essay on Philanthropy No 14*. Indiana University Center on Philanthropy.

McClure, Kevin R. 2009. "Madrasas and Pakistan's Education Agenda: Western Media Misrepresentation and Policy Recommendations." *International Journal of Educational Development* 29 (4): 334–41. https://doi.org/10.1016/j.ijedudev.2009.01.003

McCully, George. 2008. *Philanthropy Reconsidered: Private Initiatives Public Good Quality of Life*. AuthorHouse.

McCully, George. 2012. "'Philanthropy,' 'Nonprofits,' and the IRS Master Data File for Massachusetts." *Conversations On Philanthropy* 9-Law&Philanthropy. https:// www .convers ationsonph ilanthropy .org/ journal -contribution/ philanthropy -nonprofits-and-the-irs-master-data-file-for-massachusetts/

Mishler, Alan, Erin Smith Crabb, Susannah Paletz, Brook Hefright, and Ewa Golonka. 2015. "Using Structural Topic Modeling to Detect Events and Cluster Twitter Users in the Ukrainian Crisis." In *HCI International 2015—Posters' Extended Abstracts*, edited by Constantine Stephanidis, 639–44. Communications in Computer and Information Science. Springer International Publishing. https://doi.org/10.1007/978 - 3-319-21380-4_108

Mittermaier, Amira. 2019. *Giving to God: Islamic Charity in Revolutionary Times*. University of California Press.

Mittermaier, Amira. 2021. "Non-Compassionate Care: A View from an Islamic Charity Organization." *Contemporary Islam* 15 (2): 139–52. https://doi.org/10.1007/s11562 -020-00457-9

Mohamed, Besheer. 2018. "New Estimates Show U.S. Muslim Population Continues to Grow." *Pew Research Center* (blog). 2018. https://www.pewresearch.org/short -reads/2018/01/03/new-estimates-show-u-s-muslim-population-continues-to-grow/

Morey, Maribel. 2021. *White Philanthropy: Carnegie Corporation's* An American Dilemma *and the Making of a White World Order*. University of North Carolina Press.

Moumtaz, Nada. 2018. "'Is the Family Waqf a Religious Institution?' Charity, Religion, and Economy in French Mandate Lebanon." *Islamic Law and Society* 25 (1–2): 37–77.

Moumtaz, Nada. 2021. *God's Property: Islam, Charity, and the Modern State*. University of California Press.

Mueller, Tim B. 2013. "The Rockefeller Foundation, the Social Sciences, and the Humanities in the Cold War." *Journal of Cold War Studies* 15 (3): 108–35.

Murphy, Anne. 2004. *Mobilising Seva ("Service"): Modes of Sikh Diasporic Action*. Brill. https://doi.org/10.1163/9789047401407_018

Nicholls, Matthew. 2020. "Eurgetism." In *Encyclopedia Brittanica*. Chicago: Encyclopædia Britannica, Inc. https://www.britannica.com/topic/euergetism

North American Islamic Trust (NAIT). n.d. "About NAIT." Accessed May 26, 2023. https://nait.net/index.php/about-nait/about

Nyazee, Imran Ahsan Khan. 2000. *Islamic Jurisprudence: Uṣūl Al-Fiqh.* International Institute of Islamic Thought.

Obadare, Ebenezer, and Kelly Krawczyk. 2022. "Civil Society and Philanthropy in Africa: Parallels, Paradoxes and Promise." *Nonprofit and Voluntary Sector Quarterly* 51 (1): 76–102. https://doi.org/10.1177/08997640211057453

Oberauer, Norbert. 2008. "'Fantastic Charities': The Transformation of 'Waqf' Practice in Colonial Zanzibar." *Islamic Law and Society* 15 (3): 315–70.

Oberauer, Norbert. 2013. "Early Doctrines on Waqf Revisited: The Evolution of Islamic Endowment Law in the 2nd Century AH." *Islamic Law and Society* 20 (1–2): 1–47. https://doi.org/10.1163/15685195–0001A0001

O'Leary, Amy. 2012. "Christian Leaders Are Powerhouses on Twitter." *The New York Times*, June 2, 2012, sec. Technology. https://www.nytimes.com/2012/06/02/technology/christian-leaders-are-powerhouses-on-twitter.html

"Online Zakat Calculator." n.d. Islamic Relief USA. Accessed May 27, 2023. https://irusa.org/zakat-calculator/

Opwis, Felicitas. 2005. "Maṣlaḥa in Contemporary Islamic Legal Theory." *Islamic Law and Society* 12 (2): 182–223.

Orbay, Kayhan. 2017. "Imperial Waqfs within the Ottoman Waqf System." *Endowment Studies* 1 (2): 135–53. https://doi.org/10.1163/24685968-00102002

Osei, Dennis Boahene, and Imhotep Paul Alagidede. 2022. "What Drives Formal and Informal Cash and In-Kind Giving, and Volunteering, and Is the Relationship Substitutable or Complementary? Evidence from Ghana." *Journal of Human Behavior in the Social Environment* 0 (0): 1–28. https://doi.org/10.1080/10911359.2022.2072041

Osili, Una, and Çağla Ökten. 2015. "Giving in Indonesia: A Culture of Philanthropy Rooted in Islamic Tradition." In *The Palgrave Handbook of Global Philanthropy*, edited by P. Wiepking and F. Handy. Palgrave Macmillan UK. https://doi.org/10.1057/978113734153

"Our Scholars." n.d. Islamic Relief USA. Accessed May 27, 2023. https://irusa.org/our-scholars/

Payton, Robert L., and Michael P. Moody. 2008. *Understanding Philanthropy: Its Meaning and Mission.* Indiana University Press.

Penner, Louis, Michael T. Brannick, Shannon Webb, and Patrick Connell. 2005. "Effects on Volunteering of the September 11, 2001, Attacks: An Archival Analysis1." *Journal of Applied Social Psychology* 35 (7): 1333–60. https://doi.org/10.1111/j.1559-1816.2005.tb02173.x

Petersen, Marie Juul. 2012. "Islamizing Aid: Transnational Muslim NGOs After 9.11." *Voluntas: International Journal of Voluntary and Nonprofit Organizations* 23 (1): 126–55.

Peucker, Mario. 2016. *Muslim Citizenship in Liberal Democracies: Civic and Political Participation in the West.* Springer.

Pew. 2010. "Tolerance and Tension: Islam and Christianity in Sub-Saharan Africa." *Pew Research Center's Religion & Public Life Project* (blog). April 15, 2010. https://www.pewforum.org/2010/04/15/executive-summary-islam-and-christianity-in-sub-saharan-africa/

Pew Research Center. 2011. "The Future of the Global Muslim Population." Pew Research Center's Forum on Religion & Public Life. https://www.pewresearch.org/religion/2011/01/27/the-future-of-the-global-muslim-population/

Pew Research Center. 2012. "Commitment to Islam," August 9, 2012. https://www
    .pewforum .org/ 2012/ 08/ 09/ the -worlds -muslims -unity -and -diversity -2 -religious
    -commitment/
Phillips, Susan D., and Tobias Jung. 2016. "Introduction: A New 'New' Philanthropy:
    From Impetus to Impact." In *The Routledge Companion to Philanthropy*, 5–34.
    Routledge.
Pope, Ricky J., and Shawn T. Flanigan. 2013. "Revolution for Breakfast: Intersections
    of Activism, Service, and Violence in the Black Panther Party's Community
    Service Programs." *Social Justice Research* 26 (4): 445–70. https://doi.org/10.1007/
    s11211–013–0197–8
Powell, Russell. 2009. "Zakat: Drawing Insights for Legal Theory and Economic
    Policy from Islamic Jurisprudence." https://papers.ssrn.com/abstract=1351024
Powers, David S. 1989. "Orientalism, Colonialism, and Legal History: The Attack on
    Muslim Family Endowments in Algeria and India." *Comparative Studies in Society
    and History* 31 (3): 535–71.
Qaradawi, Yusuf Al. 2020a. *Fiqh al-Zakah: Volume 1: A Comparative Study of Zakah,
    Regulations and Philosophy in The Light of Quran And Sunnah*. Translated by
    Monzer Kahf. Dar ul Thaqafah.
Qaradawi, Yusuf Al. 2020b. *Fiqh al-Zakah: Volume 2: A Comparative Study of Zakah,
    Regulations and Philosophy in the Light of Quran and Sunnah*. Translated by
    Monzer Kahf. Dar ul Thaqafah.
Quinn, Kevin M., Burt L. Monroe, Michael Colaresi, Michael H. Crespin, and Dragomir
    R. Radev. 2010. "How to Analyze Political Attention with Minimal Assumptions
    and Costs." *American Journal of Political Science* 54 (1): 209–28. https://doi.org/10
    .1111/j.1540-5907.2009.00427.x
Quran Dictionary. 2017. The Quranic Arabic Corpus. 2017. https://corpus.quran.com/
    qurandictionary.jsp?q=Sdq
Rashid, Mamunur, M. Kabir Hassan, How Shi Min, and GM Wali Ullah. 2017.
    "Reporting of Zakat and Charitable Activities in Islamic Banks: Theory and Practice
    in a Multi-Cultural Setting." In *Handbook of Empirical Research on Islam and
    Economic Life*, 163–92. Edward Elgar Publishing.
Richardson, G. (2004). "Islamic Law and Zakat: Waqf Resources in Pakistan." In *Islam
    and Social Policy*, edited by S. P. Heyneman, 156–80. Vanderbilt University Press.
Ridlwan, Ahmad, and Raditya Sukmana. 2018. "The Determinant Factors of Motivation
    to Pay Zakat in Regional Amil Zakat Agency of East Java." *KARSA: Journal of
    Social and Islamic Culture* 25 (January): 334. https://doi.org/10.19105/karsa.v25i2
    .1398
Robinson, Cabeiri deBergh. 2013. *Body of Victim, Body of Warrior: Refugee Families
    and the Making of Kashmiri Jihadists*. University of California Press.
Rooney, Patrick M. 2010. "Dispelling Common Beliefs about Giving to Religious
    Institutions in the United States." In *Religious Giving: For Love of God*, edited by
    David H. Smith, 1–27. Indiana University Press.
Ross, Jack. 1974. "The Voluntary Associations of Ancient Jews: A Neglected Research
    Area." *Journal of Voluntary Action Research* 3 (3–4): 84–90. https://doi.org/10.11
    77/089976407400300309
Roy, Olivier. 1994. *The Failure of Political Islam*. Harvard University Press.
Sachar Committee Report. 2006. "Social, Economic and Educational Status of the
    Muslim Community of India." https:// www .minorityaffairs .gov .in/ sites/ default/
    files/ sachar_comm.pdf

Saiti, Buerhan, Adama Dembele, and Mehmet Bulut. 2021. "The Global Cash Waqf: A Tool against Poverty in Muslim Countries." *Qualitative Research in Financial Markets* 13 (3): 277–94. https://doi.org/10.1108/QRFM-05-2020-0085

Salamon, Lester M. 1999. *America's Nonprofit Sector: A Primer*. Foundation Center Publishing.

Salamon, Lester M., and Helmut K. Anheier. 1992. "In Search of the Non-Profit Sector. I: The Question of Definitions." *Voluntas: International Journal of Voluntary and Nonprofit Organizations* 3 (2): 125–51. https://doi.org/10.1007/BF01397770

Sanjuán, Alejandro García. 2007. *Till God Inherits the Earth: Islamic Pious Endowments in Al-Andalus (9–15th Centuries)*. Brill.

Santos, Márcia R. C., Raul M. S. Laureano, and Sérgio Moro. 2019. "Unveiling Research Trends for Organizational Reputation in the Nonprofit Sector." *VOLUNTAS: International Journal of Voluntary and Nonprofit Organizations*, January. https://doi .org/10.1007/s11266-018-00055-7

Saxton, Gregory D., and Lili Wang. 2014. "The Social Network Effect: The Determinants of Giving Through Social Media." *Nonprofit and Voluntary Sector Quarterly* 43 (5): 850–68. https://doi.org/10.1177/0899764013485159

Schacht, Joseph. 1953. "Early Doctrines on Waqf." In *FUAD KÖPRÜLÜ ARMAĞANI*, 444–52. Istanbul: Osman Yalçin Matbaasi.

Schaeublin, Emanuel. 2019. "Islam in Face-to-Face Interaction: Direct Zakat Giving in Nablus (Palestine)." *Contemporary Levant* 4 (2): 122–40. https://doi.org/10.1080/20581831.2019.1651559

Schoenblum, Jeffrey A. 1999. "The Role of Legal Doctrine in the Decline of the Islamic Waqf: A Comparison with the Trust." *Vanderbilt Journal of Transnational Law* 32 (4): 1191–1228.

Scott, David. 1999. *Refashioning Futures*. Princeton University Press.

Scott, David. 2004. *Conscripts of Modernity: The Tragedy of Colonial Enlightenment*. Duke University Press.

Scurlock, Rebecca, Nives Dolsak, and Aseem Prakash. 2020. "Recovering from Scandals: Twitter Coverage of Oxfam and Save the Children Scandals." *VOLUNTAS: International Journal of Voluntary and Nonprofit Organizations* 31 (1): 94–110. https://doi.org/10.1007/s11266-019-00148-x

Serôdio, Paulo M., Martin McKee, and David Stuckler. 2018. "Coca-Cola—A Model of Transparency in Research Partnerships? A Network Analysis of Coca-Cola's Research Funding (2008–2016)." *Public Health Nutrition* 21 (9): 1594–1607. https://doi.org/10.1017/S136898001700307X

Shaham, Ron. 1991. "Christian and Jewish 'Waqf' in Palestine during the Late Ottoman Period." *Bulletin of the School of Oriental and African Studies, University of London* 54 (3): 460–72.

Shaham, Ron. 2000. "Masters, Their Freed Slaves, and the Waqf in Egypt (Eighteenth–Twentieth Centuries)." *Journal of the Economic and Social History of the Orient* 43 (2): 162–88.

Shatzmiller, Maya. 2001. "Islamic Institutions and Property Rights: The Case of the 'Public Good' Waqf." *Journal of the Economic and Social History of the Orient* 44 (1): 44–74.

Shaul Bar Nissim, Hanna. 2019. "'New Diaspora Philanthropy'? The Philanthropy of the UJA-Federation of New York Toward Israel." *Nonprofit and Voluntary Sector Quarterly* 48 (4): 839–58. https://doi.org/10.1177/0899764019828048

Siddiqui, Shariq A. 2010. "Giving in the Way of God: Muslim Philanthropy in the United States." In *Religious Giving: For Love of God*, edited by David H. Smith, 28–48. Indiana University Press.

Siddiqui, Shariq A. 2013. "Myth vs Reality: Muslim American Philanthropy since 9/11." In *Religion in Philanthropic Organizations: Family, Friend, Foe?*, edited by Thomas J. Davis. 2nd edition. Indiana University Press. http://www.jstor.org/stable/ j.cttl6gz9gg

Siddiqui, Shariq A. 2022. "Muslim Philanthropy: Living Beyond a Western Definition." *Voluntary Sector Review*, 1–17.

Siddiqui, Shariq A., and David A. Campbell. 2023. *Philanthropy in the Muslim World: Majority and Minority Muslim Communities*. Edward Elgar Publishing, Incorporated.

Siddiqui, Shariq A., and Rafeel Wasif. 2021. "Muslim American Giving 2021." Muslim Philanthropy Initiative, Lilly Family School of Philanthropy.

Siddiqui, Shariq A., Rafeel Wasif, Micah Hughes, Afshan Parlberg, and Zeeshan Noor. 2022. "Muslim American Zakat Report 2022." Report. Muslim Philanthropy Initiative, Lilly Family School of Philanthropy. https:// scholarworks .iupui .edu/ handle/1805/28468

Singer, Amy. 2008. *Charity in Islamic Societies*. Cambridge University Press.

Singer, Amy. 2018. "The Politics of Philanthropy." *Journal of Muslim Philanthropy & Civil Society* 2 (1): 2–20.

Slama, Martin. 2018. "Practising Islam through Social Media in Indonesia." *Indonesia and the Malay World* 46 (134): 1–4. https://doi.org/10.1080/13639811.2018.1416798

Slovic, Paul, Daniel Västfjäll, Arvid Erlandsson, and Robin Gregory. 2017. "Iconic Photographs and the Ebb and Flow of Empathic Response to Humanitarian Disasters." *Proceedings of the National Academy of Sciences* 114 (4): 640–44. https://doi.org/10.1073/pnas.1613977114

Soskis, Benjamin. 2014. "Both More and No More: The Historical Split between Charity and Philanthropy." Hudson Institute. October 14, 2014. http://www.hudson .org/ research/ 10723 -both -more -and -no -more -the -historical -split -between -charity -and-philanthropy

Suárez, David F., Kelly Husted, and Andreu Casas. 2018. "Community Foundations as Advocates: Social Change Discourse in the Philanthropic Sector." *Interest Groups & Advocacy* 7 (3): 206–32. https://doi.org/10.1057/s41309-018-0039-z

Sulek, Marty. 2010a. "On the Modern Meaning of Philanthropy." *Nonprofit and Voluntary Sector Quarterly* 39 (2): 193–212. https:// doi .org/ 10 .1177/ 0899 764009333052

Sulek, Marty. 2010b. "On the Classical Meaning of Philanthrôpía." *Nonprofit and Voluntary Sector Quarterly* 39 (3): 385–408. https:// doi .org/ 10 .1177/ 0899 764009333050

Taniguchi, Hiromi. 2012. "The Determinants of Formal and Informal Volunteering: Evidence from the American Time Use Survey." *VOLUNTAS: International Journal of Voluntary and Nonprofit Organizations* 23 (4): 920–39. https://doi.org/10.1007/ s11266-011-9236-y

Taylor, Christopher B. 2016. "Islamic Charity and the Paradox of 'Obligated Voluntarism': A Comparison of Christian and Muslim Charitable Giving." *Maydan* (blog). November 22, 2016. https://themaydan.com/2016/11/islamic-charity-parad ox-obligated-voluntarism-comparison-christian-muslim-charitable-giving/

"The World's Muslims: Unity and Diversity." 2012. *Pew Research Center's Religion & Public Life Project* (blog). August 9, 2012. https://www.pewresearch.org/religion/2012/08/09/the-worlds-muslims-unity-and-diversity-2-religious-commitment/

Timani, Hussam S., and Loye Sekihata Ashton. 2019. "Introduction." In *Post-Christian Interreligious Liberation Theology*, edited by Hussam S. Timani and Loye Sekihata Ashton, 1–8. Springer International Publishing. https://doi.org/10.1007/978-3-030-27308-8_1

Tlemsani, Issam, and Robin Matthews. 2013. "Zakat and the Elimination of Poverty: New Perspectives." *International Journal of Information Technology and Business Management* 9 (1): 54–69.

Tunç, Esra. 2022. "An 'Otherwise' Philanthropy." Lake Institute on Faith and Giving. *Insight Newsletter* (blog). February 8, 2022. https:// lakeinstitute .org/ resource -library/ an-otherwise-philanthropy/

Turner, Richard Brent. 2013. "African Muslim Slaves and Islam in Antebellum America." In *The Cambridge Companion to American Islam*, edited by Juliane Hammer and Omid Safi, 28–44. Cambridge Companions to Religion. Cambridge University Press. https://doi.org/10.1017/CCO9781139026161.005

United Nations Development Programme. 2020. "Human Development Report 2020: The Next Frontier: Human Development and the Anthropocene." United Nations Development Programme.

Van Til, Jon. 1990. *Critical Issues in American Philanthropy: Strengthening Theory and Practice*. Wiley.

Varghese, P. Joseph. 2015. "Advocacy in Mental Health: Offering a Voice to the Voiceless." *Indian Journal of Social Psychiatry* 31 (January): 4. https://doi.org/10.4103/0971-9962.161987

Verschoor-Kirss, Alex. 2012. "Even Satan Gets Likes on Facebook: The Dynamic Interplay of Religion and Technology in Online Social Networks." https://dspace2.creighton.edu/xmlui/handle/10504/64308

Veyne, Paul. 1990. *Bread and Circuses: Historical Sociology and Political Pluralism*. Translated by Brian Pearce. The Penguin Press.

Wahb, Yousef Aly. 2023. "The Use and Misuse of Zakāh Funds by Religious Institutions in North America." *Religions* 14 (2). https://doi.org/10.3390/rel11 4020164

Wang, Lili, and Peiyao Li. 2022. "Government Assistance, Religiosity and Charitable Giving: Comparing Muslim and Non-Muslim Families in China." *Voluntary Sector Review* 13 (3): 417–35. https://doi.org/10.1332/204080521X16383852007870

Wasif, Rafeel. 2021. "Terrorists or Persecuted? The Portrayal of Islamic Nonprofits in US Newspapers Post 9/11." *VOLUNTAS: International Journal of Voluntary and Nonprofit Organizations*, February. https://doi.org/10.1007/s11266-021-00317-x

Wasif, Rafeel, and Aseem Prakash. 2017. "Do Government and Foreign Funding Influence Individual Donations to Religious Nonprofits? A Survey Experiment in Pakistan." In *Nonprofit Policy Forum* 8: 237–73. De Gruyter.

Weir, T. H., and A. Zysow. 2012. "Sadaka." In *Encyclopaedia of Islam, Second Edition*. Brill. https:// referenceworks .brillonline .com/ entries/ encyclopaedia -of -islam -2/sadaka-COM_0956

Weiss, Holger. 2020. *Muslim Faith-Based Organizations and Social Welfare in Africa*. Springer Nature.

"What Is Zakat Al-Fitr, the Special Ramadan Zakat?" n.d. Zakat Foundation of America. Accessed May 30, 2023. https://www.zakat.org/what-is-zakat-al-fitr-the -special-ramadan-zakat

"Who Can Zakat Not Be Given To?" n.d. National Zakat Foundation UK. Accessed May 26, 2023. https://nzf.org.uk/knowledge/who-can-zakat-not-be-given-to/

"Why CAIR Qualifies for Zakat." n.d. Council on American Islamic Relations. Accessed May 27, 2023. https://www.cair.com/why-cair-qualifies-for-zakat/

Wiepking, Pamala. 2021. "The Global Study of Philanthropic Behavior." *VOLUNTAS: International Journal of Voluntary and Nonprofit Organizations* 32 (2): 194–203. https://doi.org/10.1007/s11266-020-00279-6

Wilkerson, John, and Andreu Casas. 2017. "Large-Scale Computerized Text Analysis in Political Science: Opportunities and Challenges." *Annual Review of Political Science* 20 (1): 529–44. https://doi.org/10.1146/annurev-polisci-052615-025542

Wilkinson-Maposa, Susan, Alan Fowler, Ceri Oliver-Evans, and Chao Mulenga. 2005. "The Poor Philanthropist: How and Why the Poor Help Each Other." Cape Town, South Africa: UCT Graduate School of Business. http://www.thepoorphilanthropist.org/wp-content/uploads/2015/09/the_poor_philanthropist.pdf

Wilson, John. 2000. "Volunteering." *Annual Review of Sociology* 26: 215–40.

Wuthnow, Robert. 1991. *Acts of Compassion: Caring for Others and Helping Ourselves.* Princeton University Press.

Xu, Weiai (Wayne), and Gregory D. Saxton. 2019. "Does Stakeholder Engagement Pay Off on Social Media? A Social Capital Perspective." *Nonprofit and Voluntary Sector Quarterly* 48 (1): 28–49. https://doi.org/10.1177/0899764018791267

Zahrah, Muḥammad Abū. 2001. *The Four Imams: Their Lives, Works and Schools of Jurisprudence.* Dar Al-Taqwa.

"Zakat Chicago—CIOGC." n.d. The Council of Islamic Organizations of Greater Chicago. Accessed May 26, 2023. https://www.ciogc.org/zakat-chicago/

"Zakat Policy." n.d. LaunchGood. Accessed May 27, 2023a. https://www.launchgood.com/zakatpolicy

"Zakat Policy." n.d. Tayba Foundation. Accessed May 27, 2023b. https://www.taybafoundation.org/zakat-policy

"Zakat Policy and FAQs." n.d. Save The Children UK. Accessed May 26, 2023. https://www.savethechildren.org.uk/how-you-can-help/events-and-fundraising/ramadan/zakat-policy

"Zakat-Eligibility Of Research-Based Organizations." 2019. AMJA Online. May 1, 2019. https://www.amjaonline.org/fatwa/en/9991/zakat-eligibility-of-research-based-organizations

Zhou, Huiquan, and Eileen Le Han. 2019. "Striving to Be Pure: Constructing the Idea of Grassroots Philanthropy in Chinese Cyberspace." *VOLUNTAS: International Journal of Voluntary and Nonprofit Organizations* 30 (4): 709–23. https://doi.org/10.1007/s11266-018-9950-9

Zunz, Olivier. 2014. *Philanthropy in America: A History.* Princeton University Press.

Zysow, A. 2012. "Zakāt." In *Encyclopaedia of Islam, Second Edition.* Brill. https://referenceworks.brillonline.com/entries/encyclopaedia-of-islam-2/zakat-COM_1377

Index